Masculinity and Its Discontents

Offering a uniquely psychoanalytic developmental perspective on male gender identity and the sense of maleness, this book provides an in-depth analysis of the development of masculinity in childhood and its continued evolution throughout a man's life.

Drawing on classical Freudian theory, as well as on more contemporary psychoanalytic theories, this book explores early infancy and child development; preoedipal factors and the oedipal complex; the influence of parenting and the unconscious transmission of gendered factors both by mothers and by biological and symbolic fathers; the male ego ideal; social, cultural, and biological influences; the role of inherent psychic bi-genderality in the context of gender binaries; and the inherent gendered tensions and challenges experienced as an individual progresses into adult and later life. This book is original in its characterization of the male developmental trajectory as underpinned by psychoanalytic principles pertaining to conflict and inherent tensions that continue throughout the life cycle and strongly impact other areas of life. Deeply rooted in the unconscious, a man's multiply determined sense of masculinity requires deconstructing the mother, the feminine, and the other in the male psyche. As the text illustrates via clinical vignettes, an awareness and an understanding of these areas can improve the clinical work of psychoanalysts working with men who struggle with the intrinsic conflicts in their sense of maleness.

This book will be of great clinical value to psychoanalysts, psychotherapists, and other mental health practitioners, and will stimulate the thinking of scholars in such areas as gender theory, psychodynamic and sociocultural aspects of gender roles, and the changing social definition of masculinity.

Michael J. Diamond is a Training and Supervising Analyst at the Los Angeles Institute and Society for Psychoanalytic Studies. He has authored over ninety articles and chapters as well as three books, including *My Father Before Me: How Fathers and Sons Influence Each Other Throughout Their Lives* and *The Second Century of Psychoanalysis: Evolving Perspectives on Therapeutic Action* (with C. Christian). He is in private practice in Los Angeles.

Masculinity and Its Discontents

The Male Psyche and the Inherent Tensions of Maturing Manhood

Michael J. Diamond

Routledge
Taylor & Francis Group

LONDON AND NEW YORK

First published 2021
by Routledge
2 Park Square, Milton Park, Abingdon, Oxon OX14 4RN

and by Routledge
52 Vanderbilt Avenue, New York, NY 10017

Routledge is an imprint of the Taylor & Francis Group, an informa business.

British Library Cataloguing-in-Publication Data
A catalogue record for this book is available from the British Library

Library of Congress Cataloging-in-Publication Data
Names: Diamond, Michael J., 1944- author.
Title: Masculinity and its discontents : the male psyche and the inherent tensions of maturing manhood / Michael J. Diamond.
Description: New York : Routledge, 2021. | Includes bibliographical references and index. |
Identifiers: LCCN 2021000653 (print) |
LCCN 2021000654 (ebook) | ISBN 9780367724030 (hardback) |
ISBN 9780367724047 (paperback) | ISBN 9781003154662 (ebook other)
Subjects: LCSH: Masculinity. | Identity (Psychology) | Psychoanalysis.
Classification: LCC BF175.5.M37 D53 2021 (print) |
LCC BF175.5.M37 (ebook) | DDC 155.3/32--dc23
LC record available at https://lccn.loc.gov/2021000653
LC ebook record available at https://lccn.loc.gov/2021000654

ISBN: 978-0-367-72403-0 (hbk)
ISBN: 978-0-367-72404-7 (pbk)
ISBN: 978-1-003-15466-2 (ebk)

Typeset in Sabon
by MPS Limited, Dehradun

To my treasured family who enliven my life in infinite ways:
my wife, Linda, and our children, Maya and Alex

And in loving memory to the person from whom I learned the most about being a man:
my father, Moses Diamond

Contents

Author's preface

This book represents the culmination of many decades of my exploration of the realm of masculinity and the male psyche through my clinical work, writing, and interactions with and learning from many colleagues interested in gender-related issues, all of which have led to a number of previous publications. Though most of the ideas presented in this book are based on my long-term, extensive clinical and personal experience, along with those of other analysts writing in this area, nonetheless—as with so many psychoanalytic concepts and terms—many of these ideas are greatly impacted by cultural, geographical, and generational factors, as well as situated at the level of well-educated hunches.

I write this as we are living in an unprecedented time of global pandemic, which has led to political, health care, economic, and environmental instability. As well, we are experiencing worldwide protests that could lead to a reawakening in response to racism and nationwide divisiveness, and in its midst there is also a dismal failure of moral and unifying leadership. It is a time of enormous social and cultural upheaval, including fundamental changes in the ways in which gender is understood and performed.

As a psychoanalyst, I believe that, while the basic tensions inherent in navigating gender will remain a part of the human psyche, we can nonetheless observe radical and widespread changes in sociocultural notions of masculinity and femininity and in other facets of identity, including racial and ethnic constructions. Thus, the ways in which we view and experience masculinity are evolving among the younger generations, particularly millennials and those from Gen Z, and we can predict that these variations will expand upon many of the ideas discussed in this book.

In joining me in my explorations of the male psyche, the reader may be curious about the personal and professional contexts that most influence my understandings. I consider myself a cisgender male who grew up in a heteronormative, Western culture—with, of course, my own limitations and biases, despite being well versed in the relevant literature and having extensive clinical and collegial experience with both gay and straight men. Nonetheless, the predominance of the book's information relates especially to heterosexual and/or gay men, with relatively less material particularly directed toward increasingly relevant, alternative forms of sexuality that we will continue to hear and read about as well as be impacted by much more in the future.

Professionally trained as both a social scientist and psychoanalyst, I identify most strongly with the *American Independent Tradition* (initially described by Chodorow 2004), especially in its *West Coast* countenance. This one- and two-person psychoanalytic perspective of both/and, which strives to be more patient-driven than theory-focused, straddles a middle ground incorporating elements of such psychoanalytic perspectives as British Object Relations, Neo-Bionian, French, Intersubjective/Relational, and Contemporary Field Theory. While my pluralistic orientation encompasses these varied viewpoints, it is essentially grounded in the modern Freudian stance that emphasizes the body-mind interface, drives, and unconscious mental work. Readers will likely glimpse the fusing of such influences throughout the book.

My wish in offering my understandings about masculinity and the inherent tensions of the male psyche is that others will follow up my ideas with both intellectual rigor and careful clinical observation, in order to determine whether they withstand the tests of time and careful scrutiny.

Michael J. Diamond
Los Angeles, CA
Summer 2020

Acknowledgments

The understandings that have led to this book were inspired by so many psychoanalytic writers and colleagues, patients, and friends. Though I cannot do justice to all, I would like to acknowledge the influence of several analytic writers on my work in the areas of masculinity and gender, most of whom I remain in internal dialogue with (and several of whom I continue to engage with in the external world). Among the most significant for me are Steve Axelrod, Rosemary Balsam, Nancy Chodorow, Ken Corbett, Dianne Elise, Irene Fast, Gerald Fogel, Leticia Glocer Fiorini, Adrienne Harris, Donald Moss, William Pollock, Bruce Reis, John Munder Ross, and Martin Teising, among many others.

While protecting them by preserving their anonymity, I want to thank the many patients from whom I have learned so much and whom I hope to have helped in equal measure. I am thankful to so many of my colleagues at the Los Angeles Institute and Society for Psychoanalytic Studies: students and supervisees; teachers and mentors; friends, allies, and rivals—all of whom have enlivened my continuing journey along the road toward a deeper understanding of the complexities of being a man and, more important, a human being. Special thanks are also due to the many national and international colleagues who have so generously contributed to the understandings set out in this book, often through lively exchanges both in print and at various congresses over many years.

I also wish to express my gratitude to many dear friends in our field who have helped me to appreciate the unique experiences of manhood across its developmental pathways. I am especially thankful for the wisdom, playfulness, trust, and authenticity that's been shared with *Los Hombres* (*Sinceros*), a group of unique men in our profession, most of whom I've met monthly with for over twenty-five years, including Dan Minton, Robert Moradi, R. James Perkins, Loren Woodson, and the late Saul Brown. I also appreciate the many friends and colleagues who continue to encourage my writing while patiently bearing my limited availability during my recurrent writing retreats. My heartfelt thanks especially to Steve Axelrod, Joe Bobrow, Pam Dirham, Mindy and Paul Eads, Lisa Halotek, Tom Helscher, Susan Jay, Beth Kalish, John Lang, Marilyn Levin, Steve Lowe, John Lundgren, Ingrid Moeslein-Teising,

Robert Moradi, Jim Perkins, Marc Sanders, Sandy Schpoont, Deb Shaw, Alan Spivak, and Martin Teising. Finally, I am deeply and especially grateful to my dear friend and colleague Jerry Shapiro, a fellow investigator of the soul for most of my adult life and with whom I have shared so many of the feelings, thoughts, and ideas that have culminated in this book.

I am greatly indebted to my editorial assistant, Gina Atkinson, for her support, intelligence in grasping ideas, patience, and immense skill in finding the spot-on word at the right moment. I couldn't have managed the load without her gentle and straightforward manner.

Above all this book could not have been written without the support, love, and understanding of my wife, Linda, who has been my harshest critic, enthusiastic cheerleader, and understanding partner in tolerating my extensive sequestered hours spent writing. And I am grateful to our grown children, Maya and Alex, along with their partners, Mitchell and Kate, all of whom never fail to have my back, just as I have theirs. Finally, I wish to recognize the pervasive influence of my father, Moses Diamond, who inhabited a most generative sense of maleness in a kind, gentle, and loving manner, inspiring me to do the same.

1   The roots of male gender identity: an introductory overview

This chapter presents a historical overview of psychoanalytic thinking about gender and masculinity, beginning with Freud. I then present my own view, which is that the prephallic, phallic, and genital features of a man's internal experience are best understood as coexisting positions in varying, discontinuous balances that shift as a man matures, rather than representing distinct developmental phases that supersede one another in linear fashion. Other post-Freudian theoretical developments within the field are presented and discussed at length, including some key contemporary perspectives on gender. Implications for psychoanalytic treatment are discussed, as well as the concepts of *gender binaries* and *phallic logic*. I also discuss at length the *disidentification theory* and its status as a widely accepted theory of male development, after which I explain my own revisioning of this theory in light of new ways of thinking about men and masculinity that have emerged in recent decades—both in psychoanalysis and, more generally, in Western culture.

Masculinity and psychoanalysis: beyond the Freudian bedrock

Until four or more decades ago, the psychoanalytic study of male development was essentially organized around Freud's oedipal theory and the crucial idea that the boy wants to *have* his mother (Freud 1923, 1924, 1925). With Oedipus as exemplar, it was assumed that, in order to overcome castration anxieties aroused in competing with his father, the boy identifies with him, and in turn constructs the sense of his own masculine identity—namely, his sense of maleness. In short, classical oedipal theorizing centers on the boy's phylogenetically derived incestuous, competitive, and patricidal impulses accompanied by talionic castration anxieties, while essentially omitting the significance of the primacy of the other—i.e., the mother—in the earliest, prephallic realm. Before discussing this earlier realm, however, I wish to note that the underlying frailty of masculinity I will emphasize is embedded in the oedipal myth in Oedipus's being abandoned by his father, Laius, to die on a hillside, along with Oedipus's wounded feet, blinding, and late-life dependence on his daughter, Antigone.

Freud's ideas about masculinity are implicit in his drive-based descriptions of active and passive drive aims, which arguably become located in gendered terms during the phallic stage (Freud 1905), later considered the infantile genital stage (Freud 1923). During this stage, upon discovering anatomical differences between the sexes, the young child recognizes that he or she is missing an anatomical part possessed by the opposite sex and, in turn, experiences castration anxiety (the little boy) or penis envy (the little girl). Consequently, the boy's *active* infantile genital (drive) aim, then, is to do something with the object, to penetrate like a man, whereas his *passive* aim is to have something done to him, to be genitally penetrated like a woman.

However, in the equation of masculinity with activity and femininity with passivity, as exemplified in referring to the male's bedrock struggle "against his passive or feminine attitude toward another male" (Freud 1937, p. 250), as well as the boy's "*typically* masculine ... special interest in his father" (Freud 1921, p. 105, italics added), both the neglect of *prephallic vulnerability* and the *rejection of femininity* were furthered. This problematic account of masculinity was extended when Freud (ibid.) argued that the repudiation of femininity, the so-called "masculine protest," reflects a "biological fact"—which, he added, is "nothing else than castration anxiety" (pp. 252–253). As a result, gender-related forms of distress were erroneously attributed to the male's failure to repudiate femininity.

Freud believed that the male's repressed wish for the missing genital structure and its associated receptive aims and desires set the stage for men's highly conflicted *psychic bisexuality,* which opposes the work of psychoanalysis. Nonetheless, as I will argue, in order to contain and begin to symbolize the specific vulnerabilities and enigmas of gender difference, "everyone must reckon with their capacity for receptivity and thrust, accessibility and force, openness and backbone ... *the feminine and masculine within us all*" (Celenza 2010, p. 202, italics added).

This confusion between receptivity and passivity, between the masculine and the feminine, and between psychodynamics and biology, continues to collude with cultural assumptions and hinders theorizing about masculinity (as well as femininity). To be sure, Freud left us with numerous "impossible tasks," one of which "has been the conceptualization of bedrock" (Moss 2012, p. 94)—namely, the male's conflict-laden psychic bisexuality, which reflects his disposition to seek out what Freud (1905) understood to be both active and passive drive aims.

To better understand these themes and their relevance to the male developmental trajectory, let's begin by considering the earliest realm.

The prephallic realm and the male's primordial vulnerability

A key point I wish to make is that the *prephallic, phallic,* and *genital* features of a man's internal experience are best understood as coexisting positions in varying, discontinuous balances that shift as a man matures (much like the Kleinian notion of paranoid-schizoid and depressive positions), rather than representing different developmental phases that supersede one another in a linear way. A man's *primordial vulnerability,* marked by absence and lack, serves as the foundation for structuring his sense of masculinity. As a necessary fact of life, that primordial vulnerability proves integral to a fluid yet sufficiently balanced phallic/genital progression among prephallic, phallic, and genital interior positions.

Incorporating the idea of the primacy of the male's essential primordial vulnerability helps us better understand and appreciate the challenges in reworking the internal phallic and genital positions, characterized by dualities grounded in the male body accompanied by intrapsychic conflicts pertaining to penetration and receptivity, delinking and binding together, as well as renunciation and incorporation. A boy's *differentiation from* his mother and his *identification with* and *by* both mother and father, including their unconscious, rather inexplicable sexualized messages pertaining to his *maleness*—sexualized in the Freudian infantile polymorphous, pregenital sense—profoundly influence his gendered ego ideals, while his gender ambiguities are continually being reworked (Corbett 2011; Diamond 2009). Consequently, to paraphrase Freud, in order to truly understand "what men really want," we will also need to address the *prephallic* realm, wherein what I term *primordial vulnerability* resides.

Negotiating the oscillating passages between and among the prephallic, phallic, and genital positions requires accommodations to one's primordial vulnerability and incompleteness that present every male—who is inevitably born of a sexually different *other* (his mother)—with unique and lifelong challenges entailing ongoing conflict, confusion, and psychic effort. Consequently, in expanding on Freudian bedrock and preoedipal individuation, perhaps we might utilize Achilles's powerless heel barring immortality to serve as a prototype with which to better understand the formation of the originary, prephallic *allocation* (Laplanche 1992), as well as the preoedipal, narcissistic foundations of the structures of masculinity (Diamond 2004b, 2015). Although the latter will be elaborated in Chapters 2 and 3, it may be helpful to note here also that the male's phallic narcissism may help defend against the terrifying annihilation dangers associated with the young man's unrepresentable, primal, and bodily based vulnerability that, like Achilles's heel, signifies the fragility inherent in mortality.

This is aptly and movingly expressed in Stephen Dunn's (2004) poem "Achilles in Love," in which the poet describes how carefully Achilles hides his weakness inside reinforced boots, resulting in a certain invulnerability but also in a sense of aloneness, even in the company of others. Only when Achilles allows another to penetrate his defenses does he learn that love demands a degree of self-exposure.

The idea of masculinity surpassing the necessity of any repudiation or delinking, as well as overcoming constriction, inescapable confusion, and unsettling conflict, represents an impossible, fantastic, and utopian vision of an idealized masculinity that does not in fact exist. In contrast, I propose that, due to its foundation in the boy's primordial vulnerability signified by *lack, incompleteness,* and being *less than,* masculinity always needs to be proven and affirmed. This results in both hetero- and homosexual males' lifelong task of looking into metaphorical mirrors—including the analyst's mirror—to determine if they are really "men" (Moss 2012).

Implications for psychoanalytic treatment

A successful psychoanalytic process can usefully impact a man's relationship to what inexorably remains an elusive and essentially enigmatic sense of "masculinity"—the irreducible predicament of being male—with its primordial vulnerability, archaic anxieties, and psychic bisexuality. These pervasive and defining elements, when taken together, reflect what I suggest be more aptly termed *psychic bigenderality,* which I will discuss further later in this and subsequent chapters. In this respect, as I will address in Chapter 8, *the resumption of the unconscious bisexualization process, entailing ubiquitous and inescapable bigendered tensions, represents a primary aim of analytic treatment.*

In analysis, male patients delimited by the phallic, narcissistic polarity of penetrable/impenetrable ego ideals that precludes accepting the object dependence of human existence—a polarity originating in their primordial vulnerability—are forced to deal with disturbances accompanying the dismantling of male certitude, most forcibly in the arena of gender identity. However, the conundrum of masculinity can never be resolved or settled once and for all; rather, it can only be contained through partial integration. Though it may seem implausible or even utopian, when successful, a new definition of what it means to be a man can be largely reconciled with the more rigid notion of masculinity formed early on. In a man's tolerance and management of the enigmas and tensions of masculinity through the analytic process, the passage from pathological dependence and/or rigidly defensive independence can take place, and his fundamental relational nature can be fully embraced.

I will next turn briefly to the rather controversial concept of *gender* and consider its psychoanalytic history, postponing until later chapters the further discussion of various aspects of the concept.

Anatomy, destiny, and gender

Whereas Freud did *not* use the terms *gender* or *gender identity* or explore such areas, several generations of psychoanalytic theorists have grappled with gender-related issues, as well as with questions raised by Freud's original ideas on psychosexual development. *Gender* and *gender identity* (to be discussed in greater detail in Chapter 2) were introduced by the biologically oriented psychologist John Money (Money, Hampson, and Hampson 1955, 1957) and integrated into psychoanalytic thought by Robert Stoller (1964, 1968). Freud did not have the words since in the German language, *Geschlecht* means both *sex* and *gender.*

Nonetheless, the idea was not lacking for Freud, given his ongoing effort to resolve the riddle of masculinity / femininity, which he understood to be a mixture of the psychological, biological, and sociological. As I will further elaborate in the next chapter, it is noteworthy that Freud (1925), due to operating from a phallocentric perspective favoring male subjectivity, initially tackled these issues through his account of how the young child's discovery of the anatomical differences between the sexes, with the resulting castration anxiety or penis envy, influences male and female psychosexual development.

However, Freud's famous dictum that "anatomy is destiny" is no longer the linchpin of psychoanalytic gender theorizing. As I discuss in Chapter 6, research on the masculinization of the brain or lack thereof, as well as male-female genetic differences, demonstrate that several *biological variables* are related to specific gender-related traits, maturational challenges, and intrapsychic conflicts commonly experienced by males. Nonetheless, on the basis of clinical evidence, the biological givens in gender identity formation are significantly counterbalanced by what psychoanalysis emphasizes. For the boy, as I elaborate in Chapter 3, the construction of gender identity—his sense of maleness—is mainly determined by the early imprinting of the actual interactions with his primary attachment figures, including the mother's implanting of her unconscious reactions to her son's maleness; his internalized object relations; the prevailing sociocultural determinants; and most importantly, his unique, psychodynamically influenced reactions to each of these determinants, particularly as they interact with his basic biological development. The process of adopting a masculine or a feminine identity entails translations, fantasies, and identifications *with* and identifications *by* the mother (and the father) that help form psychic structure (Lacan 1949; Laplanche 1989, 1997). We might say, therefore, that with respect to his biological sex, the destiny of a boy's masculinity is based on *what he makes of the projections, internalizations, and constructions that emerge from his anatomy.*

Contemporary thinking about gender as it has been emerging over the last 30 years has resulted in an influential critique, in large measure empirically based, of Freud's phallocentric theories of male and female development (Balsam 2001, 2018, 2019; Chodorow 2012; Diamond 2020; Glocer Fiorini 2007, 2017). Freud, in collapsing the distinctions between biological sex, sexuality, and gender, "made gender crudely derivative of the anatomical differences between the sexes" (Goldner 2002, p. 63). Today's more complex gender identity paradigm untangles gender per se from sex and sexuality, and as Kulish (2000) suggests, our thinking about gender can be organized into five major interrelated areas: (1) the complexity and fluidity of gender; (2) the social construction of gender; (3) embodiment; (4) the separation of gender and object choice; and (5) normality versus marginality.

Furthermore, four major dialectics currently shape gender theory and require attention: (1) biological versus social influences; (2) nomothetic versus ideographic approaches; (3) the relationship between gender identity and desire; and (4) facilitating and limiting aspects of the male-female gender binary (Hansell 2011). I believe that working with the latter requires considerable deconstruction as well as foresight; I will discuss this in the section that follows.

Gender binaries and phallic logic

Focusing on the male-female gender binary, I would like to point out that such binary, either-or logic obfuscates the complex psychic constellations that characterize the psychic experiences of any individual man—the multiple, plural masculinities of hetero- and homosexual men—that appear in the unconscious conflicts, fears, fantasies, and resistances of our psychoanalytic patients. Regrettably, in the *phallacy of binary reasoning*, with its simple, reductive binary code of castration and *phallic logic*, a narcissistic world of *more* or *less* is characterized by have/have not, presence/absence, and yes/no reasoning; hence, a zero-sum game operates in which masculinity requires that femininity be repudiated (Figlio 2010; Laplanche 2007). Because the early cross-gender identifications tend to be repudiated with ideals based on gender bifurcation, concrete, binary, and oppositional forms of complementarity become structured in the oedipal phase (Bassin 1996; Benjamin 1996; Fast 1984, 1999).

Despite the disadvantages to binary thinking just indicated, it appears that, at least throughout Westernized cultures, gender binaries are in fact essential in order for children to create a stable foundation for their core gender identity (Hansell 1998). Owing to this early sense of security, the boy's losses in separating from his mother's orbit can give way to more nuanced, flexible, and complex gender ideals throughout life.

However, in underscoring inherent psychic bisexuality, Fogel (2006), like our Jungian colleagues, suggests that a dialectical balance between the *masculine principle* (characterized by boundaries, definitions, penetration, differentiation, and doing) and the contrasting *feminine* (represented by fluidity, receptivity, creativity, containment, integration, space, and being) is required for healthy maturation. Heenen-Wolff's (2011) careful reading of Freud's texts confirms that the "underlying bedrock" (Freud 1937, p. 252) is psychically structured bisexuality grounded in psychic identifications and distinguished from object choice. For instance, in an 1899 letter to Fliess, Freud stated that "the bisexual capacity—to desire, to love, to be able to be identified with both sexes without this first being the result of defensive processes—belongs entirely to … psychic life, in more or less unconscious fashion" (quoted in Heenen-Wolff 2011, p. 1212). In other words, "the unconscious is and remains bisexual" (p. 1217), to which I would add (and will elaborate upon in the next few chapters), *bigendered*.

I believe that this line of thinking leads back to Freud's fundamental ideas about psychic bisexuality and the child's inherent frailty, utter helplessness, or *hilflösigkeit* that we can observe in mother-infant dependency. In transcending the metaphorical phallus as the primary organizer of higher mental functioning—with its simplistic, binary logic that bifurcates receptivity and penetration, as well as passive and active—psychoanalysis is drawn back to the incomprehensible "lost feminine half" and "dark hole" in a man's inner genital position (Fogel 2006). In representing the otherness of the [m]other's subjectivity, both the feminine and maternity remain inherently enigmatic and mysterious for the male. From Freud's exclusively androcentric perspective of male subjectivity, the feminine became "the dark continent" equated with the object of *lack* (originally, the penis) and serves as the basis for the male's dread of women, whom he described as "mysterious, strange and ... apparently hostile," which produced the fear "of being weakened ... [and] infected with ... femininity" (Freud 1918, p. 198).

Disidentification theory: the post-Freudian creation of a male developmental benchmark

Contra Freud, Margaret Mahler and others influenced by her began to formulate a new way of understanding male psychology (Mahler, Pine, and Bergman 1975). Most significant were Ralph Greenson and Robert Stoller, who, in studying transsexuals (Stoller 1964, 1965, 1968), formulated what has become known as the *disidentification theory*. This hypothesis argues that in order to establish a normal, healthy sense of masculinity, the small boy must at a certain point disidentify from his mother and counteridentify with his father—a definitive benchmark in the development of his gender identity.

To support his thesis, Greenson (1968) presented the case of Lance, a "transsexual-transvestite five-and-a-half-year-old boy" whose mother "hated and disrespected her husband and men in general," while his father "was absent ... and had little if any pleasurable contact with the boy" (pp. 371–372). Employing this clinical material, clearly reflective of a quite disturbed family system, Greenson generalized that Lance's "problems in disidentifying" were both developmentally normative and extremely meaningful in understanding "realistic gender identity" formation (p. 372). Both Chodorow (1978) and Stoller (1985) later used the term *disidentification* to elaborate on the preoedipal determinants of cohesive gender identity that were tied to issues of separation from the mother.

Greenson's brief paper is quoted often, and analysts eager to better understand men and male development adopted the Greenson-Stoller hypothesis and made it the most important clinical application of preoedipal theory in the treatment of men. Critical commentary on the disidentification theory has been sparse within mainstream psychoanalysis until my own publications appeared earlier this century (Diamond 2004a, 2004b, 2006)—work partly inspired by Irene Fast's (1984, 1999) incisive observations drawn from attachment theory. Anticipating the work of mainstream psychoanalysts, Fast emphasizes real-life interactions between little boys and their mothers and fathers, while pointing to the ensuing internalizations and their impact on internal schemata. She posits that the baby boy's working models are gendered from the beginning of life, albeit *not* as a function of identification with the mother's "femaleness and femininity," but rather as a result of the particular interactions between the baby boy and his mother, as well as with his father. A sufficiently secure attachment with the boy's mother must occur—Bowlby's (1988) *secure base*—in order for the necessary transitional movement away from her to take place, which enables the little boy to return to his mother and thereby to reengage in a cross-sex relationship. Under these circumstances, "when he feels securely a member of the male community, he reengages his mother, now with a focus on sex-difference issues, himself as boy with his gender-different mother" (Fast 1999, p. 657).

I argue that the conceptual foundation for the disidentification hypothesis actually draws on several questionable formulations, including the supposition that all boys experience a "blissful symbiosis" with the mother (Mahler, Pine, and Bergman 1975) that produces something resembling *primary femininity* (Stoller 1964), requiring the boy to disidentify from his mother. This theory happens to be congruent with a dubious, unconsciously held binary view, widespread in patriarchal cultures, that masculinity is defined by its not being feminine. In other words, the most significant thing about being a man is *not* being a woman. This view has been unfortunate for both sexes but perhaps especially so for men, since gender identity, as long as it is based on the disavowal of whatever is construed as feminine, remains an unstable psychological achievement.

In fact, *disidentification* is a perplexing term—actually, a misnomer because early identifications are never simply removed or repudiated in the unconscious once and for all. Rather, the boy's early identifications with his mother and father remain significant in his psychic structure; these identifications typically play a more active and conscious role and become more accessible as he matures. Interestingly, in contrast to Greenson's vague notion, Laplanche and Pontalis define *identification* as a "psychological process whereby the subject assimilates an aspect, property, or attribute of the other and is transformed, wholly or partially, after the model the other provides. It is by means of a series of identifications that the personality is constituted and specified" (1973, p. 205).

This definition warrants emphasis because it leads us to correctly view identification as a consequence of various environmental disruptions and crises of integration. For our purposes, it is useful to realize that this level of internalization requires the establishment of a sufficiently gratifying pre-oedipal emotional tie with another human being that is stable and enduring, termed *primary identification* (Freud 1921). Consequently, particularly when there is a disruption of sufficiently gratifying emotional ties to a primary other, the earliest internalizations serve to build psychic structure as "the child reaches out to take back ... [what has been set up in the ego in the form of] ... what has been removed from him" (Loewald 1962, p. 496). Through the internalization process, renounced external objects—such as the mother whom the boy turns away from—become internal objects as the internal relationship becomes substituted for an external one.

Indeed, at least in Western cultures, there is abundant evidence that little boys do tend to move away physically from their mothers and toward their fathers (or surrogates) to establish themselves as boys among males (Abelin 1975; Gilmore 1990; Mahler, Pine, and Bergman 1975; see also Freud 1921). Nonetheless, there has been a significant departure from Greenson and Stoller's once-prevailing "protofeminine" *normative model* (Stoller 1976), in which infant boys develop in a feminine direction; hence, they would be required to "disidentify" from the feminine (and the mother) in order to achieve a sense of masculinity. Whereas Freud originally understood gender as stemming from the fact that masculinity was the natural state for both sexes—namely, *primary masculinity,* whereby girls retreat from masculinity into femininity upon discovering the lack of a penis—Greenson (1968) and Stoller (1968) proposed that boys are naturally *protofeminine* and must learn to renounce their femininity in order to achieve healthy gender identity.

Today, we recognize that there is no evidence to support such primary or protofemininity (nor primary masculinity), and neither masculinity nor femininity is considered phylogenetically innate. In contesting the model wherein boys must *disidentify with* their mothers, *repudiate* their feminine identifications, and *counteridentify* with their fathers, we recognize such forceful splitting as both theoretically and clinically problematic, as well as ultimately indicative of substantial psychopathology.

The fact that, as noted, the little boy tends to turn away from his mother and toward his father raises two important questions. First, is this turning away required for the male's normal psychological development? (Some cross-cultural data suggest otherwise.) Second, is it necessary for a boy to create a mental barrier against his contradictory desire to maintain closeness with his mother?

To answer these questions, let's consider masculinity in the clinical sphere, where we frequently encounter patients with conflicted, fragile, and damaged masculine self-images. Traditionally, these internal conditions are understood as expressions of *too little* or *too much* masculinity. Boys or men with too little masculinity are looked upon as passive, nonphallic characters largely under the sway of the negative Oedipus complex. In contrast, those with too much masculinity tend to be defensively counteridentified from their mothers, often evidencing a heightened phallic narcissism. However, when we look more closely at a young man like Seth, to be discussed in Chapter 2, we see evidence of both what might be considered too little masculinity in his overt passivity and inhibited aggression, and too much masculinity in his phallic insistence on staving off emotional experience and his terror of being penetrated (as by other men's eyes in public urinals). In short, the clinical picture is far more muddied than prevailing clinical notions of masculinity might suggest.

The pathological systems in which young men such as Seth and Jake (an adult father to be discussed in Chapter 5) are enmeshed are characteristic of families unable to successfully triangulate. An arrested or fixated sense of masculinity tends to be grounded in a pathological form of early triangulation that forecloses healthy triadic relations and oedipal resolution (Abelin 1975, 1980; Axelrod 1997; Fast 1990). Pathological forms of early triangulation are set in motion by (1) mothers who are severely misattuned to the individuation needs of their young sons; (2) fathers who are either weak and unavailable or misogynistic themselves; (3) a parental couple prone to splitting; or (4) the child's own biological constitution, temperament, and drive endowment, particularly with respect to what neuroscientists refer to as *brain and bodily masculinization* (Panksepp 1998) and what psychoanalysts broadly term *merger proneness*.

Under any or all of these circumstances, early gender identity development takes on the quality of a conflict or struggle, as Greenson suggests, and the little boy will tend to internalize the father's and/or the mother's contemptuous, devaluing attitude toward the opposite gender (though most often, such contempt is directed toward what is associated with the *feminine*). I propose that such pathological systems are characteristic of more "narcissistic families" wherein it is problematic for more than one subjectivity to exist, since either one member's subjectivity dominates or subjectivity itself is generally poorly recognized (Diamond 2004b). When this defensively based disidentification (and counteridentification) occurs in the little boy, a pathologically phallic rigidity commonly results. Thus, a kind of zero-sum game operates in which masculinity requires that femininity be relinquished. Engaging in the defenses of denial and disavowal of maternal identifications, the young boy attempts to expel from consciousness early identifications typically grounded in more pathological triangular relations.

What has been termed *femiphobia* (Ducat 2004)—an unconscious hatred and dread of the part of the self experienced as feminine—often ensues in these situations. The almost unknown word *gynephobia*, denoting a *fear of women*, may be even more apt in that it neither implies hatred of women/females nor misogyny. Regardless of the term employed, the male's repudiation of his feminine self signals a failure in optimal development and is evident in a defensively phallic organization that denies a man's "procreative capacity and nurturing possibilities" (Fast 1984, p. 73).

In contrast, when triadic relations are adequate, the boy's task in establishing a relatively healthy sense of maleness is not about overcoming protofemininity, but rather about building on the gendered schemes he has been establishing since birth through *identifications with and by* the mother and father (or their surrogates), including their attitudes toward him as a male person. Moreover, the little boy must consolidate his sense of himself as *boy* in *same-gender relationships* with his father (and males in general) that are not dominated by shame, and in *other-gender or cross-gender relations* with his mother. These key points will be discussed and explored at length in the chapters to follow.

Revisioning boys turning away from their mothers

In revising the disidentification theory, I emphasize that *masculinity is forged from the boy's earliest wishes to be both his mother and his father,* and that *these early identifications require adaptations and accommodations throughout the life span.* I argue that a male's gendered ego ideals and his sense of his masculinity, as well as the ambiguities of his gender, are continually being reworked throughout his life. Moreover, as I've suggested, the prephallic, phallic, and genital features of a man's internal experience are best understood as coexisting positions in varying, discontinuous balances that shift as a man matures, rather than as a linear developmental progression in which the genital phase supersedes the pre- and actual phallic phases per se.

To reiterate, then, under "good enough" conditions, the boy's turning away from his mother is transitional. This transitional turning away from the mother helps the boy differentiate and separate from his primary external object (Fast 1999). Consequently, an integrative-synthetic achievement is required of the developing male in order to employ his early preoedipal identifications. Again, such transitionality is not the same as the boy's *disidentifying* from his internal maternal object. Attachment research brings into psychoanalytic focus the conviction that a boy's secure sense of masculine identity develops from the quality of the boy-to-mother attachment, not their separation (Fonagy 2001). Attachment theorists refer to this as *attachment-individuation* rather than *separation-individuation* (Lyons-Ruth 1991)—which depends on the boy's having established a secure base with his gender-different mother.

In healthier, more normative forms of early gender identity development, progressive differentiation rather than opposition predominates, enabling masculinity to be founded on a reciprocal identification with an available father (or surrogate), a mother who is able to recognize and affirm her son's maleness, and a parental couple who together are able to acknowledge and love their son. As noted, a child, at any stage of development, can separate from familial objects in order to seek new relationships and redefine old ones, only *because* significant aspects of these early familial relationships (i.e., objects) have been internalized. The internalization processes at work in gender formation are complex, to be sure, but far more is known today than in Greenson's and Stoller's era. In particular, the small boy identifies with, and makes a part of his internal world, many aspects of his relationship with both his mother and his father.

In essence, then, boys do not establish their masculine identities only with their fathers; the mother's place in their masculine development is not simply to get out of the way, but rather to be present in specific ways that recognize and affirm the boy as a boy. This latter factor, along with the triadic functioning among the parenting couple and the boy himself, is a key determinant in his sexual identity development. This will be discussed in greater depth in Chapter

5, in which I emphasize that *the boy's male identity is largely built on his mother's unconscious attitudes toward his maleness, as well as on each parent's unconscious relationship to the son's gender and to that of the other parent.*

Later theoretical developments: primordial vulnerability, the male's core complex, and the father as third

Male gender theorizing evolved significantly during the last third of the twentieth century, particularly in North America. Researchers and psychoanalytic gender theorists such as Irene Fast (1984), Jessica Benjamin (1988), Nancy Chodorow (1994), Ruth Lax (1997), Gerald Fogel (1998), and James Hansell (1998), furthered our understanding of boys' earliest and subsequent sense of masculinity. Initially stimulated by Klein's (1928, 1932) theories drawn from child analysis, as well as by Klein's and Horney's (1933) recognition of boys' envy of the breast and womb, this line of thinking shifted its focus toward the male infant and the young boy's earliest experience with his mother (and, secondarily, his father). Accordingly, attention began to be redirected to the fact that, before the boy wants to *have* his mother, he wants to *be* his mother, or at least *be with* what his mother provides, i.e., her maternal nurturance.

This mother-infant focus implicitly addresses the child's radical helplessness—the *hilflösigkeit* suggestive of primordial vulnerability that is captured by Freud's (1905) prototypical image to denote the defenseless child. Entirely dependent on others for the satisfaction of his needs, the baby sucks at the formidable mother's breast. This fusional mother-infant relationship—with the infant actively taking in as recipient—provides satiety and security that sets the stage for every male's *core complex* (Glasser 1985), embodying his vulnerability in yearning to return to, in order to receive from, his mother. Freud's ideas concerning the complex identificatory mechanisms in establishing masculinity were accordingly extended to the boy's preoedipal relationship with his mother, as well as to the father's actual involvement in the early father-son dyad. In keeping with this Freudian perspective, these features in the early triadic environment are now seen as crucial to understanding male gender identity.[1]

A silently revolutionizing theoretical trend, spanning psychoanalytic schools and geographical cultures, addresses the omission of the *other's* significance in gender structure formation, both in terms of the concrete, flesh-and-blood other and the culturally based, symbolic other. For the boy, the first other is always his mother. Theorizing beyond the male protest and psychic bisexuality favored in what I consider to be the *first wave* in psychoanalytic male gender theory, and the subsequent *second wave's* privileging of disidentification and repudiation of the feminine, this contemporary, *third wave* of thinking (greatly influenced by French and contemporary North American analysts) focuses more upon *receptivity* vis-à-vis the other's primacy, while seeking to encompass the male's essential lack, yearning, and dependency contextualized by the phenomenal experience of having a male body in relation to his maternal other (Diamond 2015).

Overview of Chapter 2 through 8

In the next chapter (Chapter 2), I discuss how I conceptualize the *masculine* and the male's sense of his maleness given the mounting knowledge accumulated over the last half century. Through partially synthesizing contemporary views, I offer my integrative, developmental perspective on male gender identity. Chapter 3 explores the early childhood shaping of masculinity, whereas the next two chapters consider the respective impact of the father (Chapter 4), of the mother, and of the parenting couple on the boy's sense of maleness, in addition to the role played by the symbolic or so-called *paternal function* (Chapter 5).

Social, cultural, and biological influences on gender and masculinity are examined in Chapter 6, while Chapter 7 addresses maturing masculinity and receptivity, including the determinants of the male ego ideal and how it is often transformed during the male's midlife transition and later-life challenges. The final chapter (Chapter 8) addresses how the psychoanalytic process can facilitate a new and broadened experience of masculinity while pulling together contemporary psychoanalytic thoughts on masculinity and briefly summarizing some key points discussed earlier in the book.

Note

1 Particularly important work along these lines emerged from the writings of Abelin (1975); Blos (1985); Cath, Gurwitt, and Gunsburg (1989); Cath, Gurwitt, and Ross (1982); Greenspan (1982); and Herzog (1982a). A number of the more salient findings will be discussed in Chapters 4 and 5.

2 An integrative perspective on "masculine" gender and bigenderality

This chapter presents a partial synthesis of contemporary views of gender and masculinity. I offer an integrative, developmentally based perspective on male gender identity in which I conceptualize the *masculine* and the male's sense of his maleness in the light of mounting knowledge accumulated over the last half century. In deconstructing the *masculine,* the *feminine,* the *mother,* and the *other* in the male psyche, I examine the role of psychic *bigenderality* and the inherent tensions of gender fluidity. A key topic of the book—viewing male gender identity as a developmental trajectory rather than as inborn and "static—is discussed and elaborated. The applicability of these ideas to psychoanalytic work with men who struggle with the intrinsic conflicts in their sense of maleness is illustrated by a detailed clinical vignette.

Deconstructing the masculine: the "feminine" and the "mother" in the male psyche

Both psychoanalysis and prevailing cultural ideas about masculinity have developed substantially—almost in parallel fashion—over the past century. Each was constructed from and restricted by the masculine/feminine binary that led to a theory and practice centered on the idea that masculinity depends upon the overvaluation of phallicity and successful repudiation of the feminine. However, as I've indicated, such repudiation leads to psychic and material violence wherein the feminine is targeted both internally and externally (Diamond 2004b, 2006). Consequently, emerging psychic structure tends to be compromised for males engaging in denial and disavowal of maternal (and paternal) identifications. Rather than a normative process, moreover, I propose that sufficiently healthy psychic structuring becomes less likely when parental identifications are grounded in pathological triangular relations characteristic of families unable to help their sons successfully manage their desirous, incestuous, and murderous impulses.

As indicated in Chapter 1 in relation to the revision of the disidentification theory, I propose the key point that *repudiation should no longer be conceived as the linchpin of the masculine,* except in more pathological circumstances, and that, conversely, *receptivity and incorporation are central to a stable yet flexible sense of maleness.* In addition, unconscious, gender-related *psychic conflict*—an experienced reminder of absence and incompleteness—is fundamental.

We should keep in mind that theorizing male gender-related pathologies requires incorporating not only ideas based simply on what I alluded to in Chapter 1 as the *second wave* of psychoanalytic gender theorizing's repudiation of cross-gender identifications. The sensibility of the *third wave,* which attends to translations arising in the originary, mother-infant intersubjective dyad and subsequent internalizations and identifications, must also be incorporated in theorizing male gender-related pathologies. Furthermore, we must take account of the *unconscious bisexualization process* and the ubiquity of *bigenderality,* which is marked by *absence* and lack. These phenomena can all contribute to lifelong unconscious conundrums, conflicts, and resistances that remain the hallmark of the inherent tensions of what Nancy Chodorow (2012) terms "the psychic fault lines of masculinity" (p. 184).

Recognizing and including the place of the feminine and the mother in the male psyche—rather than their repudiation—has become an ongoing theme. Hence, within triadic reality—particularly concerning the lifelong father-son vector—rivalry, desire, and aggression are played out in the sphere of phallic/genital, sexual, and muscularly erotic life. According to this view, the binding together, linking forces of Eros and the coexisting, delinking, desexualizing destructive forces—the "aberrant" domain of the "demonic" repressed sexual unconscious (Laplanche 1989, 1997) and the upheaval caused by confronting the enigma of the other (Perelberg 2013)—become the object of focus.

This perspective recognizes that, as discussed in Chapter 1, *prephallic, phallic, and genital masculinity oscillate in the male psychic apparatus,* whereas *the unconscious impact of the male's unrepresentable infantile helplessness and dependency—his primordial vulnerability—serves to connect gender and genitalia,* reconfiguring the clear-cut biological/anatomical "destiny" of sex (Diamond 2006, 2015; Stein 2007).

Male gender identity as a developmental trajectory

Psychoanalysis and gender represent a frontier where the interpersonal, interpsychic, and intrapsychic interface in an interrelated mosaic. *Gender identity* refers to internal conviction regarding one's gender classification, which I believe arises from sequences of *unconscious messages, translations, internalizations, and identifications that intermingle the biological, social, and psychodynamic*—a crucial tenet to keep in mind as we continue our discussion of gender and gender identity. Thus, a complex compromise formation is constructed that neither develops in a linear, continuous trajectory nor is superior when normative (that is, within the largely heteronormative cultural imperatives). Indeed, to reiterate, the ambiguities and perplexities of male gender are continually being reworked across differing developmental junctions, particularly as I will discuss in Chapter 6, as sociocultural factors continue to make role expectations less rigidly gendered.

There is an interplay of centrality and marginality in any given life, and development is best understood as a theory of process and position rather than state and stage (Corbett 2001). Nonetheless, there is a developmental lag between gender theorizing and clinical approach that manifests as tension between the more abstract principles of *postmodern theory* ("theoretical gender"), on the one hand, in which the assertion of a stable, coherent identity is considered a defensive denial of gender fluidity and the inherent multiplicity in human subjectivity (Butler 1995; Chodorow 1996; Hansell 2011), and, on the other hand, a psychoanalytically based, *clinical sensibility* ("clinical gender") that views a relatively stable and coherent, binary-based gender identity as essential to mental health (Marcus and McNamara 2013).

I propose that *a healthy sense of masculine gender identity involves an ongoing, plastic process of destabilization and reconstruction at various pivotal stages throughout development.* In essence, maturing gender identity for males requires sufficient waning of the dominance of the phallic ego ideal that essentially denies gender and generational differences in the service of the narcissistic wish for unlimited sex and gender possibilities (i.e., what Fast [1984, 1990] termed *bisexual completeness,* an illusion that is more likely for boys). This less developed, phallic form of gender identity demands the disavowal of one's earliest sex and gender "inappropriate" identifications, a repudiation of what the little boy believes are the specifically feminine aspects of his relationship with his mother (Bassin 1996; Elise 1996) as well as his defensive efforts to avoid being shamefully humiliated by other males (Chodorow 2012; Kaftal 1991).

Masculine gender identity must be distinguished from *core gender identity* and from *sexual (gender) object choice. Core gender identity* refers to the sense of belonging to a biological sex and is usually established in the first year and a half of life (Stoller 1968). It is the felt conviction of being biologically male (or female) and is what I refer to when discussing the boy's maleness. Core gender identity helps establish the boundaries of one's gender and consequently enables the boy to develop his gender role identity without resorting to splitting operations between these two central facets of genderized identity. Nonetheless, core gender can no longer be taken for granted as a biological fact, nor can the "cisgender" binary be assumed as essential. It is not even the case that a child is born as belonging to one of two biological sexes; in fact, despite an individual's anatomy, some persons do not experience themselves as either male or female. In contrast, there are some young children who may be believed to exist in a third (or perhaps more than third) *trans* domain, and who may even eventually require the use of self-descriptive pronouns other than the standard *he* or *she*.

Though much remains to be learned about individuals born into this nonbinary realm, it is nonetheless true that—as Freud (1921) first observed and as others later elaborated—the father (or the surrogate *third*) plays an important role in the establishment of his child's sense of gender identity within the early triadic father-mother-child relationship (Abelin 1975; Blos 1984). In a well-functioning familial triad, such a father (or surrogate) tends to be aligned with a mother who maintains a *consistent affective relational presence* and who therefore needs neither to be repudiated nor renounced.

To reiterate, the traditional concept of core gender identity stands in contrast to what I am primarily addressing here, namely, the boy's *gender identity or sense of himself as a gendered person,* which Stoller termed *non-core gender identity,* and Person and Ovesey (1983) as well as research psychologists call *gender role identity.* This is a necessary, psychosocially constructed, and, arguably, a multigendered self that helps preserve what has been described as "the fluidity of our multifarious identifications" (Aron 1995, p. 202). This sense of masculinity, or the male's self-image as a gendered being, is far more complicated and ambiguous than maleness. It is fundamentally constructed out of the boy's early identifications with, and inscriptions by, each of his parents and, as I will suggest and elaborate further in Chapter 7, is reworked throughout a man's life, across differing developmental junctions including mid- and late-life stages.

It is particularly important to recognize that, as discussed in Chapter 1, the relationship between the prephallic, phallic, and the genital features of a man's masculinity is continually being reworked, evoking distinct challenges at key developmental junctures. These challenges emerge particularly during the oedipal and latency phases, in adolescence and young adulthood, and again in mid- and later life. Though I won't examine in detail each of these critical junctures, it is pertinent nonetheless to note the main gender identity-related factors operating throughout these other phases, as I will discuss in most of the subsequent chapters.

Deconstructing the feminine: the place of the other in the male's sense of maleness

In order to better understand both the *feminine* and the *masculine,* it is important to note that most of the newer ideas serve to *supplement* rather than replace traditional and still-useful concepts pertaining to sexuality, drives, compromise formations, and unconscious fantasies, all of which exist in the enigmatic realm of sexual and gender differences (during today's period of significant cultural change). Binary dichotomies are not eliminated—they remain in every individual psyche, embedded in language and culture—but the more reductive, classical equations insisting upon the masculine/feminine, active/passive, and penetrating/receptive polarities are today yielding to contradictory and more complex ways of thinking about the feminine, particularly as considerable gender fluidity is becoming more discernible. It seems inevitable that current psychoanalytic thinking will continue to help redress the imbalance so that males (as well as females) can be situated within a more inclusive coupling that includes both *potency*, in its *penetrative* and *generative* forms, and an *active receptivity and permeability*.

Sexed and gendered subjectivity is *always* "constituted in tension" (Glocer Fiorini 2017, p. 169)—that is, the internally experienced sensations of sex and gender often conflict with unconsciously (and consciously) carried, socially constructed gender categories that reflect a *different order*. In short, gender is always marked by "tension between the internal sense of gender identity and the social structures of gender" (Schiller 2018, p. 243). Consequently, I will offer some additional ideas that may help further the efforts of both male and female analysts to bear the inherent tensions related to *feminine* and *masculine*, as well as to the differences between the sexes. In advancing beyond the restricting dualisms of phallic logic, my aim is that analysts may become better able to increase their ability to listen to each patient's unique conflicts around sex and gender.

Contemporary analytic thinking—inspired by the unique and vital contributions of such analysts as Leticia Glocer Fiorini (2007, 2017, 2019) and Rosemary Balsam (2001, 2018, 2019), among many others—has brought several facets of the feminine into clearer focus. The biologically and bodily based experience of femininity is no longer situated in opposition to the constructed feminine, which is more reductively theorized as based on the experience of *lack* (Diamond 2020). Within the binary dialectic wherein no final synthesis is within reach (Scarfone 2019), the masculine/feminine polarity tends to be located at the border between nature and culture. Consequently, nuanced consideration of the *feminine* (and the *masculine*) must include biologically *sexed bodies*, *gender assignment* at birth, multiple *identifications*, *bisexual fantasies*, fields of *desire*, *varied object choices*, and changing *gender roles*.

Gender, despite being assigned at birth as a result of the sexed body, is *always* subject to other determinants, which might be elaborated in terms of the female or male body, multiple identifications, bisexual fantasies, fluid gender roles, and variations in object choice. In short, while the masculine/feminine binary always remains inherent in the psyche as a result of language and culture, *feminine subjectivity* inevitably surmounts this essential dualism, so that our conception of the feminine in both females and males continues to evolve. Balsam (2019) suggests this entails not only operating in binary terms, but also incorporating the polarities into even greater complexities. In this fashion, the role and importance of *the feminine in the male psyche* and its impact on maturing masculinity have been emphasized in recent decades (Diamond 2006, 2009, 2020; Fogel 1998). That said, the *experience* of the feminine within a female is likely to be quite different from that within a male.

A crucial shift in our understanding of female development and the feminine was brought about through Stoller's (1976) elaboration of the concept of *primary femininity,* producing greater recognition of little girls' knowledge of their bodies. Rather than viewing the female as *lacking*, it can be argued that the "lack" was actually located more definitively in theory itself.[1]

Because primary femininity rests upon unconscious fantasies about interior spaces, Balsam's (2001, 2019) writings have helped move us into the domain of *post-phallocentric* imagery and the significance of the female body, as well as of post-binary logics, in order to free the body and its mental representations. Consequently, it is no longer so easy to locate bodily *thrusting power* as male, for example, or *receptive cavities* as female. Symbols of fierceness, aggression, and thrust can also apply to the feminine without a resort to phallic imagery and masculine principles.

In focusing on the mother-infant dyad, many authors have noted that primary feminine identifications are somatic experiences, and that the earliest sense of the feminine may arise from the spaciousness of the insides of the mother's genitalia, along with the primitive, embodied fantasies and identifications that are generated in the mother-daughter dyad. By dint of the uniqueness of internal space in the female body, the female genitalia create occasions for unconscious invasion fantasies. For many women, unconscious fantasies of invasion and unrelenting bodily pain may also be tied to what becomes part of the sense of femaleness or feminine gender identity; thus, both male and female analysts may be called upon to suffer—rather helplessly—patients' unconscious fantasies of invasion and unrelenting bodily pain (Ellman 2019). Then again, the inside of the birthing mother's body contains an *other* who must be attended to for her own and the other's survival. Arguably, then, this vital *other within the self*—what Kristeva (2019) calls "the self outside the self, *the outside-of-oneself in the* self" (p. 4, italics added)—has enormous epigenetic implications for signifying the feminine, both for the female and the male.

Before elaborating this, I'd like to note that there has been a tendency to tie the rather androcentric idea of female identity to maternity itself—a tendency whereby "woman-mother-nature" is inherently equated with a view of women (and the feminine) as abiding by a primal "law of the species" in the wish to reproduce (Blanck-Cereijido 2019). For instance, in alluding to the feminine in the male analyst, a male colleague asked me if this referred to "lactating in the countertransference"! Regardless, women and the feminine are said to belong to the sensory world of instincts while remaining outside the symbolic order. Of course, the wish to be a mother is overdetermined, and the impact on the female psyche of technological changes in birthing, including assisted reproduction and surrogacy as well as infertility, requires complex understandings.[2]

These ideas that stem largely from feminist-oriented psychoanalysts suggest that the very concept of gender polarities must be rethought. At the forefront of this endeavor, Balsam (2018) has markedly challenged "the underlying severe sexed-gender polarities that were accentuated in the old Freudian and early twentieth-century schemata" (p. 21), which set up either/or binary gender propositions—abstract, generalized (phantasized) masculine-feminine conflicts as implied by "feminine" receptivity, on the one hand, and "masculine," phallic omnipotence, on the other. In contrast, just as she and, in an earlier era, Winnicott (1971) proposed, I, too, have observed that varied gender integrations emerge from work in the transference, which I discuss further in Chapter 8.

For instance, despite the prevailing conception of receptivity as a feminine property, it is obvious that men, too, need such putative *female receptivity*—since without this capacity to receive and take in maternal contact and nurturance (mother's "milk") from the penetrating breast (or bottle), the helpless male infant cannot survive. Can we not utilize the concept of receptivity itself in other than a value-laden, sexed gender image? Both male analysts (Diamond 2009, 2015; Fogel 1998) and female analysts (Balsam 2018; Kestenberg 1968; Schiller 2018) argue persuasively that there is a *male interior space*, an inner path to *male receptivity* that involves cavities such as the mouth, lips, anus, testicular sac, or inner-body spaces, just as *female receptivity* may involve the mouth, lips, and vagina.

The word *femininity* (Elise 1997; Kulish 2000), like *masculinity* (Moss 2012), is a socially value-laden term, which, unless used quite specifically, is "pretty much useless for modern theory building" (Balsam 2018, p. 28). Consequently, rather than adopting the traditional Freudian construction that splits masculinity and femininity into *agency*, with the associated contrast of (phallic) power to *passivity* that lacks such potency, we might think of "disillusioning femininity" to free up female generativity as "potency and power" (Schiller 2018, p. 243). Despite its elusiveness, nonetheless, I will attempt to use the term *feminine* rather specifically when considering its place within the male analyst in the subsequent case, as well as in Chapter 8—particularly in addressing both male and female analysts' functioning within the analytic process.

I will now present a clinical vignette to illustrate the applicability of some of these ideas in working psychoanalytically with males who, partly due to difficulties integrating the *feminine* within, struggle with their sense of maleness.

The case of Seth: integrating the emerging viewpoint[3]

The case of Seth shows how masculinity is constructed in relation to both mother and father and the impact on the young boy of these earliest identifications *with* and *by* the essential others. In what follows, I place emphasis on this patient's early identification with the attitude of each of his parents toward his maleness, and in particular, on the transference and countertransference implications of the analyst's relationship to his own (bi-)gender fluidity.

Seth, an intelligent twenty-two-year-old professional rock musician, was troubled by somatic problems, including headaches and chronic back pain. In addition, he hadn't been able to urinate in the presence of other men at public urinals since he was fourteen. When he strapped on his guitar, Seth was the model of a "cool" male icon, but beneath the bravado he struggled with feeling sufficiently "masculine," carrying a sense of humiliation in having felt like a "sissy" since early childhood. He had been sexually active since his early teens, and when beginning treatment, he had been in a relationship of several years with a slightly older female musician whom he described as "like a guy, a tough, unemotional chick needing neither foreplay nor tenderness." He also told me that without a girlfriend he felt overwhelmed by shame and worried that he was weak and inferior, using alcohol and drugs to manage these painful feelings.

Seth was an only child of parents who had separated when he was four and divorced when he was seven. His highly narcissistic father, prone to tantrums and impulsive action, had maintained an extremely ambivalent relationship with Seth. Prior to and following the divorce, he had carried on extramarital affairs and subsequently remarried twice. Nonetheless, Seth experienced his father as highly dependent on him, often describing Seth as his "best and closest friend." Disparaging Seth's mother, he would caution Seth to be careful because "all women are out to use men."

Seth's mother, whom he remained close to while viewing as "very doting," had never remarried or apparently even dated since the divorce. She opposed his having girlfriends and discouraged him from learning to drive—a decidedly limiting predicament for a young man living in Los Angeles. Seth discovered that she had breast-fed him well past his third birthday, conceivably indicative of her difficulty separating from him. Much like Seth's misogynous father, though in a more restrained manner, she was highly critical of her former spouse and contemptuous of men in general.

During our early sessions, Seth felt lost, and his obsessive philosophizing and intellectualizing were often difficult to bear in our thrice-weekly sessions. Nonetheless, I felt something was keeping me from drifting too far away from him, and I soon recognized that his early transference hinted that he was "falling in love" with me. In return, I experienced this sweet though troubled young man with affection while holding him in my gaze. I began to look forward to seeing him, despite the tedious and distancing nature of our early sessions, and gradually he became able to allow me closer.

Sometimes a little boy lost, other times a confused teenager, Seth initially seemed to be coming to me for a feeding that required little of me but to be present and attentive to him, holding him in my gaze. With another patient

I may have experienced myself as being more like a mother holding her baby in a maternal gaze, but with Seth something else was happening. Though quite ineffable, an indisputably masculine ambience was alive as he relentlessly spoke of his efforts to define himself in his world. At the same time, he would watch me carefully while tentatively stating, "You do know what I mean."

Seth next talked about the physical closeness he had once shared with his father. In noticing how closely he seemed to be watching my face, I imagined that his desire to engage me was very much related to the way a son beckons his father to wrestle or roughhouse in order to experience their bodily presences joined together in their full and aggressively masculine forms. I sensed he was looking at me as a young boy resolutely looks to his father for affirmation by discerning his own maleness reflected back. This "isogender attachment" (Blos 1985) or "homoerotic identificatory love" (Benjamin 1991) seemed necessary in order for Seth to establish his masculine identity. It is noteworthy that my countertransference—and others in which I endeavored to appreciate how I was being acted on by my patient—were useful in helping me to understand what was occurring, and to fashion my interventions.

Seth's words were like gestures inviting my nonverbal engagement with him, and I understood these longings to be a manifestation of his *father hunger* (Herzog 2001) for a particular kind of paternal figure. I realized in time that this desperately sought-after strong man, neither so dependent on him nor demeaning of femininity, was needed to help Seth recognize his masculinity in relation to himself, to other men, and to women without having to disavow his interior world and its powerful maternal internalizations. Seth desired to find in me the man who would help him feel, as he put it, "okay to be who I really am." In paying close attention to my own experience, using it as a guide to both recognizing and interpreting Seth's transference needs, I found myself drawn toward being a kind and accepting, fatherlike mentor who could help him better understand himself and the world around him.[4]

Nonetheless, my oedipal- and preoedipal-based interpretations continued to lead us nowhere (though conveying my effort to understand him), and over time, I sought to understand how I was being acted on by my patient. For example, Seth reported a dream well into our second year in which he, as a child, was very jealous of another boy's bow and arrow set. He then found me holding his "tiny penis" and felt surprisingly "comfortable." The oedipal implications of his manifest dream were apparent in his phallic envy of the other boy's bow and arrow set and, presumably, his envy of mine. In associating to the dream, however, he was greatly surprised to find himself feeling so content in response to my holding his "tiny penis." In the uncomfortable silence after he claimed to have "no associations" to the dream, I reflected to myself on what his contentment might point to. Did it indicate Seth's longing for his mother to satisfy his preoedipal needs, including to have his maleness embraced? Might it reveal his renunciation of his own phallic-aggressive strivings (by rendering his penis as "tiny" in order to stave off his dangerous and powerful father/analyst rival)? Or could it relate to his more dyadic paternal needs, his homoerotic, isogender attachment?

Rather than offering an interpretation that might create a more distancing, intellectualized stance (for both of us), I silently waited and soon fondly recalled my own mother soothingly bathing me as a small child, and playfully washing my tiny penis while telling me a seemingly never-ending story of "little Dickie" who was learning to behave himself as a "good boy." I wondered if this memory might have some bearing on what my interpretations couldn't yet find in Seth, and eventually asked myself whether some part of Seth might have come alive in my bodily based musings. Still, by waiting rather than acting, some sort of "radical passivity" (Chetrit-Vatine 2014) or "female fecundity" (Balsam 2018) seems to have allowed me to receive what was not yet ready to be put into associative language or representation. Neither of us spoke for ten or so minutes, and I somewhat shamefully wondered if Seth and I were both avoiding analytic work, perhaps from my own more *masculine, phallic* perspective.

I waited for Seth to continue, and soon he spoke of being "traumatized" as a four-year-old boy when his father first separated from his mother. He told me how he would frequently stay at his father's apartment when his father's girlfriend spent the night. He could hear them in the adjoining bedroom "having sex, banging the walls, and making all kinds of strange and scary noises," adding that he felt very frightened while also wondering how his father could be so "insensitive." I wondered, too, as I listened further.

Later, when he was twelve, Seth had again felt "traumatized" when his father—apparently out of jealousy—made him suddenly stop seeing a male child psychologist whom he had been seeing for several years and had grown very attached to. "I think he couldn't stand how much I liked going to Dr. B," Seth said before returning to the comfortable dream image of my holding his tiny penis. His thoughts turned yet again to Dr. B, and he became angry thinking about how his father had kept him from this revered paternal figure. Seth then abruptly became preoccupied with his finances and insurance coverage for treatment, and soon we began discussing his anxiety about our work together coming to a sudden end. Seth was moved, as well as relieved, when I subsequently interpreted his wish that I become his "new Dr. B," a father figure who could remain available while recognizing what he needed in order to develop. It was becoming more apparent that my holding of his penis—though overdetermined, to be sure—indicated his longing for a stable, primarily preoedipal and dyadic paternal attachment, even an ambigendered one that allowed him to simply *be*. It proved quite beneficial to the treatment that I was now able to address this more dyadic need directly rather than focusing on the dream's conflictual, oedipal facets (and thus to take up the penis-holding as a regressive defense).

When Seth and I discussed the dream in the next session, he cried, apparently for the first time since he was a child; this is important since many men, even after years of analysis, frequently experience an internal prohibition against crying due to its association with women (Reichbart 2006). I interpreted his crying as an indication of his premature "loss" of his needed, *protective and holding father* (in the context of experiencing a newfound security with me), and this seemed to usher in a new phase in the treatment in which he felt safely held by me. In other words, he was conveying that he needed an analyst-father, much as he needed his actual father, to introduce him gradually to triadic reality in appropriate doses that would protect him from both the "too-muchness" of sudden overstimulation (manifest in his associations to hearing his father in sexual intercourse) and the precipitous loss evident in his recall of the abrupt departure of Dr. B.

I thus underscored Seth's need to experience me as the carrier of an early dyadic paternal transference in which he could feel small and yet safe in a bodily, sensual connection to a bigger male's maleness. Seth began to speak often and freely of his shame and feelings of inferiority, most notably in having to "prop up" his father by being "a happy, brainy, and non-demanding son who took care not to upset others." He had to make his penis small, so to speak, in front of other men (as at the urinal and sometimes with me) in order to create a sense of safety for himself. This compromise solution would become more evident later in our work as his phallic-aggressive wishes and positive oedipal anxieties became more amenable to interpretation. At this time, however, as his dream associations suggest, Seth greatly desired a father figure who could feel his tiny penis and recognize the little boy within who was so in need of a larger male's reciprocity. His newfound security in freely associating indicated that he was experiencing me as "propping him up," rather than as needing him to be the way his father (and analyst) wanted him to be.[5]

This period of our work highlights what I will elaborate in Chapter 4—namely, the significance of the preconflictual, dyadic father-son bond, especially in its bodily sensual form, as a significant facilitator of a boy's healthy sense of masculinity. In this respect, bows and arrows do *not* simply express phallic desire and potency; additionally, as in Cupid's pursuit of Psyche, they reflect Eros in the search for a loving connection. I took this up interpretively with Seth by commenting on his efforts to find "a father in me who, by connecting with you in our shared maleness, can help you feel more capable of dealing with the world of men and thus more comfortable in competing and freely asserting yourself."

Seth's shame around feeling insufficiently masculine quickly became our central focus. He told me that he'd regarded himself as a "sissy" since he was very young, acknowledging his forceful need to hide what he called his "emotional self" in a "dark cave" lest he experience himself as "weak and feminine." Thus, he repudiated his emotional self through an exaggerated yet aloof, "cool" masculine demeanor, covering it over with defensive phallicism. He associated the "cave" housing his emotions to the vagina; its darkness spoke to both the depth and the terror of his early bodily identification with his mother.

This material illustrates the shame-ridden danger of a boy's initial feminine identification that is formed in the primacy of the "sensual-erotic contact between infant and mother" (Wrye and Welles 1994, p. 35). In addition—and partly signified by my own reverie bringing back memories that helped me access and sufficiently tolerate the shame associated with *the feminine in myself* that seems necessary to affirm maleness—it appears that Seth was seeking to find a mother-analyst who could *affirm his little boy maleness* by holding his tiny penis in a loving, sensual manner.

As Seth recalled his father's verbally abusive berating of his mother, he began to understand his own uncompromising, sadomasochistic attacks on his emotional and needy self. He had long idealized the character of Hannibal Lechter for his "brilliant invulnerability"; only now could he recognize the internal split he had created in order to rid himself of what he regarded as soft, impure, and feminine. It wasn't just that Seth feared being castrated by his father for wanting to have his mother; on a deeper level, he was terrified that he would be annihilated for experiencing himself as being like his mother in certain ways. Indeed, for many men, losing one's penis is preferable to not existing.

Hannibal Lechter, the perfect psychopath, embodies the quintessence of phallic masculinity. But Seth was no psychopath, and he was beginning to realize that the ongoing war within himself reflected his early parental identifications—both his father's unconscious misogynist attitudes and his mother's corresponding misandry, indicated by her fear of, and contempt for, maleness. Seth had incorporated these attitudes when he was far too young to question them and hadn't been able to come to terms with these internalizations without repudiating his emotional self, in both its aggressive and its loving aspects. In fact, some time later, after becoming openly angry with me, Seth was surprised to discover that "nothing had fallen apart between us."

During the third year of treatment, Seth dreamt that he was playing a piano in a friend's house, only to become overwhelmed with sadness and cry uncontrollably. Embarrassed, he tried to leave the room without being seen but was able neither to get up nor to stop crying. In associating, Seth remembered how, as a small child, he loved hearing his mother play the piano. His uncontrollable crying reminded him of being overcome with feelings of loss as he recalled his maternal grandfather's death, his parents' separation, and his mother's subsequent depression. The sad longing in the dream seemed familiar, and he realized that the piano playing represented something that had once been very comforting and important to him. While opening himself to the sadness and longing that he had long sought to disavow, he realized that this emotional memory attached to his mother was very much inside him and, as he put it, "most definitely a part of me that I somehow lost along the way."[6]

In reclaiming the disavowed, we were now able to explore Seth's attraction to, and terror of, "feminine" women, as well as his "repulsion" to touching his mother. I helped him recognize his positive oedipal yearnings in the context of his father's distant but powerful presence, as well as his defenses against his desires and rivalrous impulses. Seth's capacity to experience competition without requiring defensive submission was increasing, and in sharing his longing to be seen as a "real man" by other guys throughout the next year, he presented numerous dreams in which his aggression was no longer so inhibited, and in which he frankly displayed his phallic equipment. Though still rather cautious, he was beginning to more easily express his aggression in everyday life. He was becoming more open with his male friends and commenced a relationship with a woman with whom he could comfortably reveal his "most personal feelings."

The material was becoming more conflict-laden, and my interpretations were focused on his wishes for, and defenses against, his assertiveness and aggression. For example, he dreamt he was playing tennis with his father, unable to return the older man's powerful volleys. He then compared their rackets and discovered that his father's was cracked at the top. In discussing his associations to this dream, Seth recognized his competitive feelings and aggressive wishes to "crack" his father (though less consciously to "crack" his analyst). His aggression was palpable as he spoke of feeling he had been a "mechanical man" for so long, surviving by "swallowing" his emotions.

We could soon discuss his fascination with Hannibal Lechter as a compromise function reflecting both his terror of being cannibalized in his maleness and his desire to be the devouring male figure himself. A major change in the nature of our work was under way. Seth began to challenge and even chastise me, often rather playfully, about my fees, my schedule, and ultimately my limitations and "cracks." For instance, on several occasions he would say something like, "So when already are you going to offer something brilliant and incisive, a Hannibal Lechter-like statement that ties everything together?"

Toward the end of our work together, Seth brought in a series of dreams involving urinals. In one dream, despite feeling uncomfortably exposed, he was using an unusually shaped public urinal, an expression of his long-standing desire to freely urinate in public. At an adjacent urinal, a very masculine man who had been squatting like a woman, aggressively stood up and shouted, "I am a man!" Seth then assertively and freely pissed into a urinal that no longer seemed so oddly shaped. In analyzing the dream, Seth reflected on his growing comfort with his maleness, including his aggressive feelings. He understood that his pissing in the urinal had felt like an attack on other men, and in recognizing the extent of his inhibited aggression, he wondered aloud, "What the hell is so bad anyway about wanting to win the pissing contests!" Seth was integrating what had been split apart—in other words, the *woman inside* him could begin to coexist alongside the *emerging man*. Seth was increasingly able to play his mother's piano, feel his sadness, and still display his *piss and vinegar* (i.e., express his manliness and aggression in the world around him).

Brief case discussion

This material illustrates that a young man often requires extensive support in integrating his earliest identifications with each parent (though, of course, a parent's impact on the child goes well beyond the issue of identification). For Seth, these identifications caused him difficulty not so much because he failed to disidentify from his mother or counteridentify with his father, but rather because of the nature of the particular identifications that he unconsciously carried forward—identifications that reflected problematic gendered attitudes and beliefs.[7] His father did not offer his son a more suitable paternal object to identify with, one who as a "genital" father could locate maleness within the matrix of a relationship, of modulated aggressive and loving affect, and of a stable emotional connection to women.

Seth's inhibited aggression toward his desperately needed father rendered him submissive since his father's mentorship in the realm of instinct and emotion was strikingly lacking. Without an available and mature father—both as a *flesh-and-blood actual presence* of the same gender and as a *symbolic function* per se—Seth grew up feeling as if he had been left stranded. He couldn't identify with a healthy man (i.e., an adult one) and was at a loss to understand how he could find his maleness in relation to his mother. Moreover, his mother's unconscious limitations in recognizing and sanctioning her boy's maleness complicated the loss. As a result, Seth predictably created a rigid, either/or version of masculinity whereby he had to ferociously repudiate every emotional feminine quality, including his feelings for his mother, in order to feel masculine. No wonder he idealized Hannibal Lechter—the impenetrable man.

Considerable analytic assistance was required in order for Seth to establish an internal cease-fire and an ongoing dialogue among his gendered internal objects. As his inner battle lessened, he found that both his masculine and his feminine sides were available rather than forbidden; thus, he could appreciate his maleness in its essential emotional and nongendered as well as multigendered diversity. In this respect, the case supports the classical idea that "a man's neurosis may be rooted in being unable to adapt to his femininity" (Wisdom 1983, p. 166).

I believe that, in order to appreciate his maleness in its essential emotional and nongendered diversity—that is, his *not being of* the binary while *living in* it—Seth needed my analytic help in establishing an ongoing dialogue between his gendered (or, more accurately, his *multigendered*) internal objects. And as I hope to have illustrated, this required my finding a way to access my own feminine or *matricial* space (Chetrit-Vatine 2014) through a *generative form of waiting* that may have necessitated tolerating my own shame in exploring the space within—namely, a space that included little-boy memories of being soothingly, playfully, and excitedly bathed by my mother.

To be precise, what was called for, as I will revisit in Chapter 8, was my bearing the tensions required when adopting what I think of as a more *fluid gender* within myself in order to receive Seth's gendered otherness in an emotionally alive way; this entailed my identifying with both a little boy and a loving mother. Though the mutative mechanism remains complicated, I believe that the male analyst's ability to find the *feminine other* within himself, often through countertransference memories or reveries, can help our male patients (as well as female ones, though perhaps by finding the contra-gendered other within) to detoxify their own shame and thereby more easily inhabit their bigenderality. Likewise, the female analyst working with male patients (and with female ones) frequently needs to access the *masculine other* within herself.

As a brief coda, I might add that, although I treated Seth more than twenty years ago, I had a dream with elements related to him while writing about this case very recently. In the dream, I was scheduled to be video-taped for an interview that surprisingly was to take place in a men's public restroom. I was placed in a chair in front of the urinals. However, I was anxious to be situated at the side of a particular urinal, perhaps to appear and to perform at my best. Interestingly, I awoke thinking about how much of my life as a heterosexual man has required great care in revealing—or perhaps more accurately, in navigating or even disguising—what might *not* be so easily acceptable in the phallocentric, binary world of gendered appearances. Indeed, in a point I will return to in the book's denouement (in Chapter 8), despite whatever gender fluidity has been attained, perhaps we are all destined to fail in our unique ways of performing gender.

Notes

1 This more classical, phallocentric view prevailed until such ideas crossed the Atlantic and were embraced by the wider psychoanalytic community. Nonetheless, earlier European analysts, such as Jones (1935) and Klein (1928), had already addressed the female child's knowledge of her unique anatomy. Concurrently with Stoller's work, Roy Schafer (1974) published a brilliant essay delineating flaws in Freud's theorizing of women that did injustice "to both his psychoanalytic method and his clinical findings" (p. 459). Subsequent psychoanalytic ideas about primary femininity have "vitalized both clinical treatment and psychoanalytic theory for women and men" (Goodman 2019, p. 87).

2 Moreover, as Glocer Fiorini (2007, 2017) and others, including me (Diamond 2017b), have suggested, even the "third," necessary to separate the child from the mother, need not be the father or a surrogate male assuming the purported *paternal function*, since this role can clearly exist independently of the person who

exercises it and can be performed by the mother herself or even by another woman as partner to the mother.

3 Selected aspects of the analytic work with Seth have previously been discussed (see Diamond 2004b, 2006, 2020).

4 At other times, in attending to the role relationship that Seth was unconsciously trying to establish (Sandler 1976), I found myself to be more of a mother figure who could support Seth's masculine tendencies by recognizing his phallic-aggressive strivings and male-related activities. Most often, however, in the paternal transference, I was experienced (and experienced myself) as a fatherly presence not needing to prove that only I was allowed to be a big, phallic man. In these circumstances, I often intuitively felt it best to allow Seth to formulate his own interpretation when it was already experience-near for him, rather than my putting it into words for him.

5 As I've noted, Seth's struggles with his phallic and aggressive strivings, his conflicted wishes to display his phallic equipment, and his defenses against exhibiting his own intact, potent phallus are clearly implied in the clinical material. These issues would come to the forefront of the interpretive work as the treatment progressed. By following Seth's associations, tracking my countertransference attitudes as a guide to his transference desires, and keeping our work experience-near, I deduced that it was best to take up this material in terms of his efforts to discover his dyadic father within preoedipal reality. By doing so, I discovered that the oedipal could eventually be navigated. In fact, only later in our work was Seth able to make contact with and constructively use my interpretations of the danger of his aggressive impulses, his rivalrous feelings toward me, and his defenses against them. In short, his envy of the bow and arrow reflected his coveting of a penis as a substitute for lacking real contact with a loving, protective father. Thus, I believe that he needed to feel my bigger penis supporting his smaller one before he could fully experience and bear his envy and aggression within triadic reality. However, in reflecting further in terms of psychic bigenderality (as elaborated in Chapter 8), perhaps through tolerating both the shame and satisfactions of living with my own bigendered tensions, might this have made it more possible for Seth to access what his shame had cordoned off? Though the actual mechanism is unclear, it does seem that something relatively unformed was becoming formed and accessible to verbal representation.

6 As I suggested in Chapter 1 and will elaborate on in Chapter 3, this sort of disavowal of a male's maternal identifications is quite common, particularly when the identifications are grounded in more pathological frameworks.

7 Facets of the internalization processes involved in each boy's unique struggle to differentiate from his mother are exemplified in Seth's case. As I detail in Chapters 3, 4, and 5, every boy's separation from the world of his mother is a complex process involving the interaction of biological and psychosocial factors, particularly upon the disruptive arrival of sexuality that results in considerable intrapsychic conflict, elaboration, and defense. Undoubtedly, this occurs for most boys in part because it also represents the loss of innocence in the relationship with the mother—the so-called *death of infancy* (Bollas 2000), wherein the mother-as-comforter becomes the mother-as-sex-object. The presence of a father or surrogate third able to carry the paternal function helps mitigate the disruption's potentially traumatic impact.

3   The shaping of masculinity in early childhood

Here, I define the terms *phallic* and *genital* and discuss why this distinction is important in considering male gender identity and development. I explore male development starting from inception and birth, noting that the male infant's vulnerability, present long before words and symbolization are possible, is fundamentally unrepresentable and nonsymbolizable. Male development during the phallic phase and beyond is discussed as well, and I note the persistence of certain aspects of phase-based intrapsychic structures throughout life, and how these may be adaptive or maladaptive depending on the individual's ensuing psychic structure and overall mental health. The seminal issue for most men is how early, preoedipal phallic narcissism and phallic omnipotence can be integrated into an ongoing and evolving sense of masculinity.

Phallicity versus genitality

A brief word on terminology: in using the terms *phallic* and *genital*, I am referring to a specific orientation, typically manifest in a cluster of traits, which psychoanalysis views as originating from early psychosexual, libidinal development. From the classical psychosexual standpoint, the *phallic phase,* preceded by the oral and anal phases, is a pregenital period beginning at about two years of age and extending into the oedipal phase, during which the phallus is the primary erogenous zone. Freud (1923) describes this "infantile genital organization" as reflecting "a primacy of the phallus" rather than of the genitals (p. 142). The phase comprises two subphases: phallic narcissism (or phallic exhibitionism), characterized by self-satisfaction based on overestimation of the penis, exhibitionistic desires to gain attention, and dyadic relations, and the later phallic-oedipal phase proper, with its triangular configuration, idealization of oedipal objects promoting phallic omnipotence, and heightened castration anxieties (Edgcumbe and Burgner 1975).

Throughout the entire phallic phase, the high valuation of the penis is manifest in phallic pride with its associated desires and anxieties. Figuratively speaking, extending, thrusting, and penetrating become paramount, along with the associated personality traits of assertiveness, aggression, strength, and potency.

The residue of this phallic taste for controlling, conquering, and vanquishing may remain in adulthood while serving quite adaptive functions (for example, in the contemporary, still largely male "warrior" world of high finance, business, and industry). However, this adaptive residue must be balanced by a maturing sense of otherness that enables such phallic strivings to be expressed more progressively in mutual play within transitional space where *the other* is taken into account (rather than, for example, in such forms as incest and murder). An expanded, more creative matrix for connection can be established when the male psyche is able to reunite and link impulses to penetrate and conquer with those to be penetrated and contained (Elise 1996, 2001).

The *genital phase* is considered the final stage in instinctual libidinal development, representing what has been called *genital primacy* (Freud 1905). Genital primacy does not equate, however, with the mere capacity for orgastic functioning; genital, taken beyond psychosexual theory, is used broadly to reflect the male's capacity to attach equal importance to his own and his partner's satisfaction. Moreover, as suggested in Chapter 2, there is an interiorized, culturally minimized dimension of genital masculinity pertaining to the inner body and testicles, the inner genital space, that reflects the more open, spatial, and receptive aspects of male psychic experience, which may be misleadingly described as *feminine*.

Maturing, healthy genitality is characterized by the attenuation of the anxieties pertaining to masculine inner space and the associated psychic sensibilities. Penetration and receptivity, as well as intrusion and inclusion, are its hallmarks. Genital aims for connection and the recognition of others in their uniqueness and subjectivity (i.e., *otherness*) are a manifestation of this postambivalent integration of phallic propensities in the service of reality. This achievement represents an ethical cornerstone of developed manhood in Western culture—namely, a level of generativity and responsibility that sociologists term *guardianship* (Seidman and Frank 2019). As I discussed in Chapter 2, this facet of *the other within the self* may be construed within the cultural binary as *the feminine* inside the male psyche—which may be experienced by the more phallic-based male as something that is *other* residing in his conflicted sense of maleness.

Prephallic masculinity/prephallic vulnerability

The distinctly bodily derived, psychosexual terms *phallic* and *genital* refer to specific, individually constructed mental orientations or positions creatively deployed and reworked within an individual throughout the developmental trajectory. These positions are typically manifest in a cluster of traits, which originate from early libidinal development beginning in the *fundamental anthropological situation* (Laplanche 1989, 1997)—namely, the infant's *prephallic* helplessness and asymmetrical relation to the implantation of the mother's perplexing sexual messages that he is incapable of translating. This radical helplessness produces a *primordial discord* at the heart of the human infant (Lacan 1949) that I believe becomes the primal source of defensive operations, as well as of "all moral motives" (Freud 1895, p. 318), and yet remains forever unrepresentable.

As I've noted, the *phallic phase* refers to that infantile genital stage (prior to the genital phase itself) beginning at about two years of age that extends into the oedipal phase, during which the phallus is the primary erogenous zone. In my first chapter, however, I proposed that what transpires *prior to the phallic stage* (i.e., during the oral and anal phases that are distinctly prephallic) reflects the *primordial and determinative nature* of male-specific vulnerability pertaining to subsequent gender-related structures. In fact, when more traumatic mother-infant relations are manifest, annihilation fears can be traced to prenatal patterns that continue throughout early childhood. Phallic rigidities then often serve to stave off more primary, unrepresentable, and weakly contained terrors.

To reiterate, the primordial and essential frailty of masculinity is inherent in Freud's (1905) image of the helpless, dependent child sucking at the mother's breast—which provides satiety and security that, once lost, is forever longed for and sought. This fact establishes the *core complex* for the male born of woman, consisting of an ever-present, absolute vulnerability in the wish to return to her (in order to receive from her) and the accompanying terror of this longing in its unconscious association with being possessed by and annihilated by the omnipotent mother (Glasser 1985).

Present long before words and symbolization are possible, *the male infant's vulnerability is fundamentally unrepresentable and nonsymbolizable*—a radical helplessness perhaps best captured by Bion's (1965) term, the *formless infinite.* My use of the term *primordial* signifies this *archaic and primitive, primary form of the boy's vulnerability vis-à-vis his originary object in their archaic matrix.* The French metapsychological tradition considers such primitiveness as belonging to the *other scene,* namely, the unconscious that remains atemporal by definition (Kristeva 2014). Attempts at representation are removed from the phenomenon itself and are never fully integrated, remaining inescapably elusive.

From the narcissistic point of view, both girls and boys feel painfully incomplete as a result of the helplessness (*hilflösigkeit*) built into their originary relationship. However, the powerful character of the primitive maternal imago—the mother as omnipotent, active, and phallic (in her penetrating attribute)—has a particular impact on boys for several reasons stemming from both psychodynamics and biology. From a psychodynamic perspective, the stages of the boy's primary identification with the maternal feminine and the subsequent separation/individuation-based losses associated with his mothering object become particularly traumatic.

Because the boy's unconscious identification with the lost maternal object is always with an object that is *different from* rather than *similar to,* the deferred action of *nachträglichkeit* (or *après-coup*) that begins to take hold during the separation phase is inevitably more disruptive for him than for the girl (whose discord is mitigated through her bodily identification with mother).[1] Nonetheless, primary repression renders the boy incapable of representing both the otherness and the terrifying anxieties in relation to the unrepresentable facets of maternity, namely, the *erotico-maternal feminine* (Cournut 1998). Soon enough, however, through the phallic order, these terrifying anxieties are sufficiently repressed and contained.

It is noteworthy, however, that there does seem to be a male, gender-specific *biological* sensitivity to maternal caregiving and a greater vulnerability to maternal psychopathology. In general, as I will discuss further in Chapter 6, recent neuroscientific findings suggest that infant boys, in contrast to girls, suffer their incompleteness within the maternal dyad more severely, whereas their maturational timetable remains slower.

Phallicity and its bodily and psychic vicissitudes

I hold that phallic ambitions, propensities, and energies are utilized, integrated, and transformed throughout a male's development, and that these phallic features of internal life will play an important role in his adaptively expressing and experiencing his masculinity. A male's defensive phallicity, however, frequently reflects regressive tendencies in an otherwise healthy personality; alternatively, it may indicate more rigid characterological distortions based on primitive defensive operations employed to protect his fragile, inflexible masculine gender identity. In the latter case, the so-called *phallic character* is characterized by exhibitionistic self-display, haughty reserve, a regarding of the penis as an instrument of aggression (rather than love), recklessness, misogyny, and an excessive need to display one's potency.

Such pathology, indicative of what more recently is called "toxic masculinity," can manifest at various developmental junctures, though it is traditionally understood as regressively based on oedipal-phase anxieties (Jones 1933). This is evident in adult men, particularly in mid- and later life (as I discuss in Chapter 7), who persist in defining themselves by conquest, sexual potency, and aggression when relational needs, a greater appreciation of otherness, and reflectivity might otherwise come to the fore.

The little boy, wishing to replicate the original experience of satisfaction at the mother's breast, relies on primary processing to mingle an unrepresentable, initial bodily experience and a nascent idea with a represented, visible, erectable, and comprehensible external part of his own body through which his desired object—namely, the lost breast, missing mother, or fusional *jouissance*—is imagined as attainable. In other words, the little boy's traumatic loss of the paradise of the originary, highly gratifying relationship with his mother predisposes him to create a phallic self-image to regain control of the object now experienced as quite separate from his ego (Chasseguet-Smirgel 1976, 1984).

Accordingly, the phallic image provides him with an illusory way to win his mother's love—a triumph apparently reflected by the gleam in his mother's eyes—and, as his mother's all-conquering hero, he becomes focused on activity and agency, the phallic conquest of the world, in order to stave off loss and chaos. Therefore, the phallus—based on the binary distinction between having and not having—is relegated to the deeper unconscious, partially representing the lost breast while also signifying his *inherently unrepresentable vulnerability*. The little boy omnipotently forms the adaptive and defensive illusion of "the supremacy of his own masculine equipment" (Manninen 1992, p. 25). In short, *phallic monism*—the belief that the penis is *the* sexual organ—comes to guard against any recognition of lack or deficiency. The masculine *phallic ego ideal* is thus based on the boy's unconscious denial of differentiation in the service of his grandiose wish to maintain the unlimited possibility inherent in the omnipotent, idealized union with his maternal object.

Such phallic monism, originally established during the anal-sadistic stage, results from the visibility of the penis (and its micturition), which is founded upon this stage's reliance on comparison, measurement, and the outward orientation of phallic sensations and discharges of male sexuality. Perhaps it is set in motion by virtue of the phylogenic fact that, in assuming the upright stance, humans lost a visual reference of the external feminine genital organs; thus, through *phallic logic,* this visual inaccessibility has been elevated to the "major universal signifier of presence/absence" (Laplanche 2007, p. 217). I suggest that the male's frequent quasi-obsession with seeing female body parts, generally evident in the importance of *looking* to satisfy erotic as well as lascivious desires—and too easily pathologized simply as part-object relating—in some measure reflects the absence of early female genital sightedness.

By focusing on an external, visible organ, the penis—rather than coenesthetic sensations that produce more unsettling anxieties—the boy is helped along as he enters the phallic phase via the use of externalization and denial of the "insides" (Kestenberg 1968). Accordingly, he shifts from inside to outside, and his inner genital sensations are externalized upon the phallus to protect against archaically feared attacks—and, as I submit, against unrepresentable primordial anxieties.

Lacanian-influenced French analysts posited that the term *phallus*, signifying a false completeness and narcissistic, illusory wholeness, describes a grandiose focus initially employed to assuage differentiation anxieties and less accessible annihilation terrors (Grunberger 1964). The phallus becomes the symbol of invulnerability—a permanently erect monolith of masculine omnipotence—manically defending against the depressive and persecutory dangers of experiencing the lack of an all-too-separate but still needed, desired, and all-satisfying maternal object to transform the discord of infantile helplessness.

In resisting fusion with the mother and the subsequent attraction of incest, albeit expressing what has been sacrificed, the phallus in phallic-narcissistic psychic retreat comes to deny the so-called "facts of life" (Money-Kyrle 1968). This commences for the phallic-phase child with the denial of the nascent sense of his or her own mortality as signified by the experience of being different and therefore *incomplete*. In the male, the absolute, radical vulnerability in his helplessness—mortality as a fact of life—can thus be dissociated through the construction of the phallic infla-tion fantasy. Existing in the unconscious as a basic position representing an impenetrable state of completeness (Birksted-Breen 1996; Grunberger 1964), the phallus fuels the paradisaical fantasy of being "*beyond* the human condition ... without need," which can prevent experiencing the intrinsic lack that permits passage into the triadic realm of the Symbolic order, wherein the paternal metaphor—the "Law of the Father"—can endure (Lacan 1949, p. 650, italics added).

Against this backdrop, as observed in certain unreachable patients who rely on omnipotence, impenetrability, and massive projective identification, taking in good supplies from the analyst is prevented. In any case, the male's fan-tasized lack of vulnerability, as well as the illusory supremacy of his male endowment and frequent obsession with penis size—illustrated by the so-called *little penis complex* (Horney 1932), which is apparent at the end of this chapter in my case example of Brad—is unconsciously linked with terrifying anxieties pertaining to this fundamental lack or absence. Projective mechan-isms prevail whereby "the other lacks all, I lack nothing" (Moss 2012, p. 35).

Throughout the entire phallic phase, the high valuation of the penis is manifest in phallic pride with its associated desires and anxieties. The pri-macy of the body and manifestations of infantile sexuality—too often neglected by contemporary theorists—produce urges to penetrate and im-pose one's self into that which is other.[2] Interestingly, infantile genital de-velopment closely parallels the morphology of the sexual organs, wherein psychic experience is anchored in the "ground plan of the body" (Erikson 1950, p. 108). For instance, preadolescent sex differences in block play indicate that for boys, height, downfall, and strong motion in constructing towers, buildings, and streets prevail along a high-low axis that is *intrusive* (rather than inclusive) in character.

As I've noted, then, extending, thrusting, and penetrating—figuratively speaking—become paramount, along with the associated personality traits of assertiveness, aggression, strength, and potency in the realization of one's desire. Moreover, the boy's primordial vulnerability becomes anatomically anchored in his observable and erectable genital organ and accompanying testicles, which in their visible exposure are particularly vulnerable to attack from outside, and hence concretized in castration fears. The prephallic precursors of such cas-tration anxieties that are triggered by oedipal conflicts are often accessed (in a retroactive, après-coup fashion) in even more alarming fragmentation and annihilation terrors that derive from the boy's primordial vulnerability.

In functioning from the fanciful yet heroic position of the phallic ego ideal, there tends to be a confusion between the penis as an object of *phallic narcissism* and as an object of *Eros or relational connection* (Braunschweig and Fain 1978). The hazard of phallic masculinity in its forever unreachable demands is that a hypermasculine, illusory image of phallic manhood constitutes a narcissistic end in itself—for example, in the constant urge to assert oneself impressively, rather than serving more creative purposes that require integrating phallic and genital ego ideals.

Understanding and simply being (rather than doing) seem threatening, and as a result, compulsively driven, manic activity dominates, as illustrated by the case of Brad, with which I conclude this chapter.

Phallic narcissism

As Freud indicated, phallic narcissism begins as a natural, adaptive process to mitigate the small boy's experience of loss and envy. The boy's traumatic loss of the paradise of the earliest, highly gratifying relationship with his mother predisposes him to create a phallic image of himself in relation to the world in order to regain control of the object now experienced as quite separate from his ego. When a contemptuous, devaluing attitude toward women is present in the father, the little boy will extend this and frequently evidence a heightened phallic narcissism. Moreover, such defensive masculinity is commonly rooted in a painful loss of dependency and love, as well as in an intense envy of the mother founded on a humiliating, narcissistic wounding (Lax 1997).

I would like to emphasize that the seminal issue for most men is how early, preoedipal phallic narcissism and phallic omnipotence—with their roots in the infant's prephallic, primordial vulnerability—can be integrated into an ongoing and evolving sense of masculinity (Diamond 2015). Unfortunately, for some men without an opportunity for a maturing ego ideal that integrates the phallic ego ideal with the genital ego ideal (represented by the internalized genital father), phallicism in the form of a hypermasculine, phallic image of manhood becomes psychically urgent in order to achieve the missing psychic cohesion. Phallic behavior becomes largely compensatory and constitutes a narcissistic end in itself, as in the constant urge to assert oneself impressively, rather than serving more creative purposes.[3]

This reliance on a more exclusively phallic ego ideal underlies the stereotypical "male obsession" whereby "only by conquering the world can one conquer the mother" (Manninen 1992, p. 7). This hypermasculine phallic image of manhood, additionally, frequently conceals the unavailability of the preoedipal "genital" father, who serves as the keystone for healthy male-to-male identity formation (Ross 1986). With respect to the "little man" of childhood, the extent of the boy's phallicism in search of narcissistic completeness greatly influences his ability to accept oedipal reality. In the end, oedipal mastery requires a boy's realization of his own limitations and becoming content with something less than an idealized, narcissistic wholeness.

In brief, then, when things go awry, the phallic ego ideal becomes needed in order to manage narcissistic anxieties arising in the complex reality of gender differentiation. True differentiation is denied, while penetration offers the promise of transcendence of vulnerability, limitation, and dependence. Under these circumstances, phallic masculinity is arrested, the phallic ego ideal dominates, and the sense of phallic urgency is paramount. This phallic form of repudiating early maternal identifications—by which maleness and masculinity are defined in the negative as *not female*—creates an unconscious *gender ossification* that often becomes manifest later as gender confusion or rigid, defensive certainty. The *phallocentric male* defensively operates as if his phallus is all that he has to make him masculine, and under these conditions, development of the *genital ego ideal,* whereby antithetical intrapsychic elements can be reunited—as, for example, between *autonomy* and *connection*—is thwarted (Diamond 2004b).[4]

The resulting male gender identifications are more fragile than flexible, partly because they are formed out of conflicted, unconscious wishes to embrace and embody one's repudiated feminine identifications in the *wish to be complete.* I find Butler's (1995) discussion of this *renunciation* intriguing; she argued that the phallic ego ideal for the boy demands that he disavow his lost connections and identifications with his earliest preoedipal opposite-sexed object—namely, his mother—in addition to requiring such disavowal with his same-sexed object—his father, because of the homoerotic bond.[5] I believe that the continuing repudiation of one's earliest sex and gender "inappropriate" identifications with both the preoedipal mother and the father is largely responsible for men's unconscious gender ossification in the form of either gender confusion or rigid certainty. Moreover, such gender ossification can represent the pursuit of a gender ideal based on a central fantasy about the existence of a forever elusive *masculine essence.*

As I will elaborate in Chapter 7, such arrested phallic narcissism or defensive phallicity (in contrast to a more adaptive phallicity with its suitable penile pride that fuels creative, purposeful activity in childhood and young adulthood) ultimately becomes a persistent obstacle to young adult and midlife growth and development and is evident in the fragmentation anxieties and sense of shame that are evoked whenever a stable masculine identity cannot be maintained. In the male's ongoing challenge of navigating the phallic-genital dialectic, many men experience a psychic, life-and-death struggle to close off the narcissistic gender wound in order to fortify their fragile masculinity. Moreover, with serious psychopathology, powerful, phallic-narcissistic defenses against psychic reality involve the repudiation of the other. Such repudiation, as evident in Brad's case discussed later in this chapter, is necessary to maintain a precariously gendered self, rigidly defending against homoerotics, psychic bisexuality/bigenderality, and thirdness, and is marked by absence, loss, and being *less than.*

In contrast, as I will elaborate further in the chapters to follow, I stress the importance of healthy, adaptive phallicism in contrast to arrested phallicism in the male's expression of self. In short, *healthy phallicism* is based primarily on what classical psychoanalysis refers to as neutralization, sublimation, and integration of the grandiose strivings of phallic narcissism or exhibitionism, as well as phallic omnipotence during the oedipal phase (Edgcumbe and Burgner 1975). Other analysts have also distinguished the healthy, adaptive form of phallic narcissism from the pathologically defensive type, especially by emphasizing the importance of the bodily component in the desire to penetrate (Corbett 2003; Schalin 1989). As I will stress in Chapter 4, this phallic development occurs mainly as a result of involved, good enough fathering (or surrogate fathering) during a boy's oedipal and latency years.

A more phallic-based, key challenge for many boys pertains to love for other males—the *forbidden love of boys* (Moss 2012), which frequently becomes foreclosed, producing a more conscious gender-refused, same-sex erotic love (Butler 1995). However, no such foreclosure exists in the unconscious, so that the male typically utilizes phallic logic, renunciation of femininity, and heteromasculinity exemplified by a phallic ego ideal to manage homoerotic anxieties, rendering him vulnerable to *obsessive-compulsive masculinity* (Jay 2007). In short, a particularized gender "performativity" often manifests in a "masculine *masquerade* of 'having' *the* phallus" (Moss 2012, p. 38, italics added).

At the same time, the repudiation or foreclosure of the desire to be loved by other males can result in isolation and internalized homophobia that generates unbearable states of mind, including suicidal and homicidal despair (ibid). Accordingly, late-adolescent boys, both straight and gay, tend to hedge about showing affection and emotional intimacy with other boys, whereas adult males often suffer from inhibitions and frustrated longings that severely limit close friendships and intimate relations with other men (Kaftal 1991). In addition, as discussed in Chapter 4 (and suggested in Endnote 5), male-to-male relationships are often restricted by anxieties pertaining to being subordinate to, shamed by, or humiliated by other males (Chodorow 2012). This contrasts with the sublimated desires and Eros evident in such typically male groupings as the military, sports teams, and work and creative alliances; here, the bonds are apparent between brothers, sons, and fathers, between close male friends and lovers, and they reveal male love for other males.[6]

The evolution toward fluid genitality

Reality-based genitality involves adaptive assertion, aggression, and modulated phallicism, whereby phallic urges are transformed into more aim-inhibited and object-recognizing forms in the relational context of mourning, acceptance, submission, and uniting with others—namely, the Kleinian idea of the *depressive position*. There is a tendency to forget that, in its essence, genitality implies a synthesis between autonomy and connection in which antithetical intrapsychic elements can be reunited.

The latter pole in this dialectic has been described more classically as reflecting the maturation of the ego ideal, whereby the ego gains its value from "aiming toward"—rather than from maintaining the illusion of "achieving" its ideal state (Chasseguet-Smirgel 1985). This progressive solution to the unappeasable longing for an unattainable ideal—i.e., *the malady of the ideal*—can thereby culminate in a sort of loving union with the world that simultaneously acknowledges the fact of the world's *otherness*.

During his oedipal phase and latency years, a boy's sense of masculinity is especially impacted by his father's (or surrogate's) beneficial use of his paternal authority, emotional regulatory capacity (particularly in modulating aggression), and admirable skill in doing things. The boy's sense of his maleness, then, is directly related to his budding ability to express and modulate aggressive and competitive urges, acquire a sense of industry, and attenuate his adaptively needed but illusory phallic omnipotence. In adolescence, as the boy differentiates from his family in seeking to develop his own identity, his masculinity is considerably influenced by his father's (or perhaps stepfather's or mother's partner's) capacity to bear the son's moving away from him (as the boy did earlier with his mother), as well as by the teenage peer group's sanctioning of his masculine identity.

Accordingly, particularly in Westernized cultures, by late adolescence and early adulthood, a young man's sense of manhood is directly tied to adult identity formation, especially influenced by his sexual prowess and ability to endure pain. In young adulthood, mentors are crucial as the young man embarks on his heroic journey to *become his own man* with his own lasting intimate relationships in the world outside his family. Thus, during his adult years, he is more likely to appraise his manhood in terms of his career success and ability to provide for his family.

I will expand upon some of these themes in Chapter 7 and in some detail in the clinical vignette of Brad that follows.

The case of Brad: rigid defenses and sadomasochism in the analytic relationship [7]

Brad, a patient in his early thirties, was an accidentally conceived only child who was born prematurely. He was forced to remain in an incubator for more than one week before returning home to his postpartum-depressed mother and his alcoholic, philandering, and generally absent father. In light of a markedly traumatic mother-infant relationship, Brad suffered extreme yet unrepresented annihilation fears; this was suggested by his aunt's informing him that, in addition to his having endured a very difficult birth process, he soon became a failure-to-thrive infant, inconsistently bottle-fed by his "unhappy" mother, who reportedly left him in his crib "crying for hours."

Brad's father abandoned the family for good when Brad was five, and he and his mother lived alone for several years until her boyfriend moved in and became physically abusive of him. Brad described his obese mother as both overly protective and "burdened" by his maleness, yet seeming to seductively valorize his genitals by often commenting on his "huge" penis. Her misandry was evident in her repeated berating of Brad's father and of men in general, whom she described as "assholes with dicks."

In short, Brad's highly invasive mother seemed to carry a phallic mask; his father abdicated the paternal function; and Brad remained masochistically tied to and identified with a seemingly omnipotent mother with a penis. Consequently, he learned to "cut off" his feelings, particularly shame and guilt, and in alexithymic fashion, was unable to recall having ever cried or even feeling sad. Although he had scant memory of his early childhood, in a later screen memory he recalled being left alone in his room, unable to find his mother, who was apparently either locked in her room or outside the house altogether.

Brad was referred for analytic work when his wife of one year abruptly divorced him. He spoke of his "disappointment" in her and in women in general, whom he described as "not very smart." He portrayed a pattern of escaping from various disappointing relationships by using pot, alcohol, and prescription medications daily to numb himself and prevent being "overloaded."

Despite Brad's manic lifestyle, unpredictable work schedule, and disavowal of neediness, we were able to establish twice- and thrice-weekly meetings. He initially spent months recounting his daily sexual conquests, while attributing his "successes" to his enormously sized penis and gigantic, brilliant mind (though a college dropout, he was a proud member of Mensa International).

He presented as a smooth-talking, tall, handsome, and fashionably dressed man who made a considerable fortune in his business. Though successful in drawing women to him, Brad lived alone in a huge house, without furniture, while spending his money on clothes, technological gadgets, excessive fitness activities, gambling, drugs, and prostitutes. Living in a narcissistic psychic retreat, he had no close friends other than those whom he "bought" to travel with him for Bacchanalia-driven weekends in Las Vegas.

Brad's prephallic vulnerability and shameful sense of inadequacy were hidden behind a manic, phallic invincibility—an easily caricatured, militant masculinity in which being "big" through action and power dominated. He overvalued the illusory supremacy of his male endowment while repudiating the feminine, evident in his locating lack in the other and his aversion to "female" characteristics. He repeatedly proclaimed that he did not want to "depend on anyone," and instead, objects (persons and otherwise) were used addictively.

The prevailing narcissistic transference that kept the vulnerability of "incompleteness" located outside him initially required little from me; I was merely a eunuch-like, mirroring presence. I eventually came to understand this as his way of staving off an intolerable exposure to his immense vulnerability through experiencing his originary neediness, helplessness, and terror of being devoured and annihilated through unconsciously submitting to the (m)other's desires.

For many months, most everything I considered saying or actually said would somehow seem wrong. I was left not knowing what to do, yet felt unable to bring my experience to life in analytic reality. Human relatedness seemed too threatening, and neither the psychic reality of a phallic dyad nor of triangular oedipal space could be settled into. Unable to mentalize Brad's weakly representable unconscious functioning, I often found myself feeling bored, tired, irritated, or emotionally absent while watching the clock. For his part, Brad often came to sessions high on pot, and he frequently cancelled sessions for meetings or social engagements. As he aptly stated, "I don't attach to people—they don't, won't, or can't love or stay with me, so I won't let myself get too involved."

We were treading on thin ice to keep the analysis surviving. On one occasion, however, late in the year, Brad began to acknowledge compartmentalizing more threatening, receptive psychic aims that he believed would lead to his being betrayed because of his "gooey center inside needing love." I could interpret this in the transference, where he kept the "gooey" vulnerable part of him in polar opposition to his idealized penetrative impulses—a disembodied, manic phallus disconnected from love, used to defend against fragmentation anxieties that were galvanized by his glimpsing what was "missing" inside.

A brief but significant entree into the fortress of Brad's tenuous psychic reality appeared early in our second year when he noticed a slight tear in the sole of my shoe. He began to laugh and then mocked me, persisting for some time in this haughty, disdainful fashion by commenting negatively on my clothing, hair, age, intelligence, and profession. Anything other than sexual conquest and success seemed futile. Despite his attacks all-too-obviously aimed at reversing his underlying terror and deep sense of shame so as to evoke my feeling ashamed and defective, I nonetheless welcomed his nascent efforts to create an object relationship. Feeling hopeful that his psychic retreat was giving way to a sense of lack and incompleteness that could come alive in the negative transference, I felt neither angry nor bored. However, as he continued to rant, I soon recalled a childhood incident in which I had felt extremely vulnerable when bullied by three larger, physically tougher boys.

An analytic space had opened slightly in which, through evacuative means, Brad's internal objects came to life in the field between us. In this case, I was the shamefully, helplessly bullied and receptive, weak, and "feminine" part of him, while he played the role of the powerfully penetrating, omnipotent object—representative of his phallic, masculine ideal—and together we engaged in an ongoing sadomasochistic, persecutory dynamic.

A small foothold appeared as I began to use my countertransference to think about what Brad could not. Although his own psychic reality remained enormously threatening, interpretive work briefly helped him recognize the inner bully that was so filled with hatred toward whatever was construed as weak and "womanly," producing a manic foreclosure of his inner life. For instance, I noted how difficult it was for him to tolerate any holes or gaps in himself, let alone in me—to bear weakness or vulnerability that he considered "feminine"—which made him fear my "penetrating" into his inner world to expose how vulnerable and easily wounded he felt. I added that perhaps he put his shame into me as a way to see if I could "suffer" it with him or for him. Not surprisingly given the stakes, Brad scoffed at my "psychoanalytic babble" because I "had nothing real to offer." Once again, he began missing numerous sessions, explaining that he would do so to get "blow jobs that are more therapeutic than what we do here."

Brad's foreclosing was exacerbated when left unanesthetized by his ad-dictive, externalizing behaviors, and any progress was unfailingly met with impenetrable phallic resistance that masked his shame and envy by eschewing an understanding that required daring to *take in* good supplies from me. After my summer holidays, despite my efforts to interpret my "abandoning" him while he experienced me as "aloof," he nonetheless hastily cut back from thrice-weekly to once-weekly sessions, took several unplanned vacations himself, and considered moving away from the area and relocating on the East Coast. Once again, interpretations seeking to represent Brad's fragile inner world, now alive in the transference, went for naught. For example, after discussing his inner bully and his tortuous master-slave psychic reality, he found a new psychopharmacologist, splitting the two of us while seeking to replace me, the inept analyst who could only "talk" rather than providing something "real" to make him "feel better."

This forward-backward tempo, marked by his repeated cancellations and increasing thoughts of relocating far away, went on for many months. However, short-lived analytic movement ensued when Brad found himself romantically involved with a transsexual—a woman with a penis (perhaps representing his longed-for phallic mother in tandem with his absent father, the "asshole with a dick"). His highly conflicted psychic bisexuality and wish *to have* and *to be* both sexes emerged, and he spoke of "wanting everything: a gorgeous, sex-crazed, six-foot stripper and 24/7 caretaker." Nonetheless, in feeling forcibly expelled from narcissistic retreat and shamefully aware of exposing his defensively constructed, tenuous masculinity—used to repudiate both his more maternal, "feminine" long-ings and his paternal hunger for the love of a man—he began to feel the pain grounded in unrepresentable terror and narcissistic mortification.

Moreover, Brad began to glimpse his own disavowed identifications with his omnipotently sadistic, phallic mother's *destructive anal penis* (Chasseguet-Smirgel 1964). His experience in becoming somewhat con-scious of these identifications, desires, and fantasies felt intolerable, how-ever, and further exploration remained foreclosed. Flight from analysis seemed imminent, and once again, Brad sought to evacuate his need for analytic help through action, destruction, and delusion. He used his manic phallus to replace any perception of what was missing inside.

Brad soon broke up with his transsexual lover and yet courageously con-tinued treatment for several more months, becoming conscious of a memory of having been molested by a female babysitter. He briefly began recounting fears of falling apart, providing a glimpse into his primordial experiences of unintegrated states and annihilation anxieties that activated omnipotent defensive operations and subsequent phallic rigidities. For a short time, his impenetrable shell no longer fit so snugly as he spoke of the loneliness and self-loathing he had felt as a "fat, ugly child with a never-ending hole inside."

Not surprisingly, however—given his use of action as a powerful defense against psychic reality—and rather sadly from my perspective, Brad resumed cancelling sessions while interviewing for jobs elsewhere. Several weeks later, he sold his home and took a position in New York, declaring that, like Icarus, he was ready to "flap my wings and fly." I gave him the name of a New York analyst (whom he did not contact), and in our last meeting, he thanked me for helping him recognize what he "lacked," reassuring us both that he would try to be more constructive with his life and would keep in touch. I did not hear from him again, however, and was left pondering the extent to which his analysis had advanced, and how one might better reach and sustain deeper contact with men whose fragile identity so strongly requires that their lack remain "lacking."

Brief case discussion

The case of Brad, while an example of a less than successful analysis, does illustrate the difficulties in working with an extremely phallic, narcissistic man governed by primitive, omnipotent manic defenses operating largely in presymbolic realms. These defenses of phallic supremacy, which served to stave off primordial vulnerabilities as well as castration anxieties, kept him (and his analyst) trapped in a sadomasochistic web that resulted in a limited analysis. Nonetheless, such a case in which concretized thinking and action continue to dominate over the course of treatment can further our understanding of the unrepresentable terrors and severe resistances associated with a male's primordial vulnerability. As in Brad's case, these resistances are likely to result in the patient's ongoing struggle to remain engaged in analytic work. Clinically, at issue is the question of how best to work in order to successfully advance the analysis given such primitive male pathology.

In the subsequent two chapters, I will consider the influences of the father, the mother, and the parental couple's impact on the boy's sense of maleness, as well as the ensuing resistances that are often encountered in analytic work with men.

Notes

1 In fearing narcissistic collapse into an "abyssal opening [topographically] beneath castration anxiety" (Kristeva 2014, p. 80), males rely on being "big" to counter maternal dependence, with its accompanying wishes and fears. Hence, it is no

coincidence that the Narcissus myth depicts Narcissus to be of the male gender and to have distinctive narcissistic conflicts.

2 Arguably, when such phallic urges to impose are poorly managed by phallo-centric men rigidly fixated in the phallic position, concrete action tends to ensue. As brought to light by the #MeToo movement, sexualized abuses that reflect "toxic masculinity," are more likely to occur, which I believe results from the ruthlessness of the phallic-driven libido left poorly modulated by genital aims—consequently, "no" comes to mean "yes," and the subjectivity of the other is eradicated.

3 In deconstructing phallicism, I emphasize its preoedipal, narcissistic foundations from both a dyadic and triadic perspective (Diamond 2004b, 2006). Such an early substructure for phallicism is evident throughout the life cycle in both the frag-mentation anxieties and the sense of shame that are evoked whenever a stable masculine identity cannot be maintained. This is quite evident in the case of Seth discussed in Chapter 2. My emphasis thus contrasts with the traditional Freudian view of phallicism, with its primary focus on exclusively triangular, oedipal dy-namics based largely on the interplay between the sexual and aggressive drives in a competitive context generating castration anxieties. Although both the pre-oedipal and oedipal basis of the sense of masculinity will remain important throughout a man's life, I stress that a mature masculinity, reflecting the attain-ment of true genitality, requires that the preoedipal, narcissistic facets of phallicism—with its roots in the infant boy's prephallic primordial vulnerability—be reworked and integrated.

4 In studying the subject of evil, Stein (2002, 2003) offered a fascinating and somewhat corresponding construction as to the psychodynamics underlying suicide-killing terrorists' ecstatic willingness to follow "God's will." Stein pro-posed that these "errant sons" regress to fuse with an archaic, cruel, and depraved father imago as an ego ideal. This love of a "corrupt father" functions to re-pudiate femininity and to "get rid of the impure, 'infidel,' soft, feminine 'godless' part of themselves" (2002, p. 415). In such a "regression to the Father," God becomes the phallus, and in this fundamentalist religious submissiveness, the repudiation of any emotional need for women offers a manic sense of liberation from becoming softened and emasculated. Thus, the radical fundamentalist group's fostering of such homoerotic merger and abjection provides the means with which to manage the more culturally uncontained anxieties otherwise manifest as painful confusion, uncertainty, and guilt.

5 However, it is noteworthy (as I will discuss in Chapter 4), the boy's disavowal of his earliest connection with his father is largely determined by the father's ca-pacity to reciprocate his son's isogender (homoerotic) attachment as well as his ability to manage his more phallic and oedipal impulses to humiliate his little, smaller boy. This is a secondary, male-to-male "fault line of masculinity" (to the repudiation of femininity) that reflects the male's vulnerability to feeling humi-liated as a "boy" in relation to other, more "adult" males (Chodorow 2012).

6 Such male-to-male desire, with its receptive aims and vulnerability, is evident in the Achilles myth that describes the shame-free relationship between Achilles and his lifelong intimate companion, Patroclus. Achilles's loyalty and love for his dear friend lead him to ignore divine prophecy and, facing certain death, he nonetheless returns to the battlefield to avenge Patroclus's death.

7 I have discussed Brad in a previous article (Diamond 2015).

4 The impact of actual and symbolic fathering on masculinity

I begin this chapter with a discussion of Freudian tenets on fathering and of the contributions of other noteworthy psychoanalytic theoreticians. I indicate the scant attention given to the father in psychoanalytic developmental theory—to the point that he is, in fact, "missing"—and I distinguish the *symbolic father* from the *actual father*. Masculinity is seen as greatly impacted by the *actual* father and his capacity to carry the *symbolic or paternal function* as the "third" in both the *attracting* and *separating* roles. These key facets of father functioning—as well as the concept of the *watchful protective* father—are described and discussed at length along genital and other lines in order to understand the father's strong influence on the son's developing gender identity, as well as the benefits of his (or his surrogate's) active involvement with his son. A clinical vignette of a man struggling to embrace fathering and the accompanying sense of adult masculinity illustrates some of these ideas.

Recovering the missing father in psychoanalytic developmental theory

In classical psychoanalytic theory, fathering is conceptualized as predominantly phylogenetically transmitted, in that *primary, primordial identification* with the father occurs in every individual male's prehistory prior to any environmental history or conflict. This vital, fundamental identification is subsequently transformed and organized around the *symbolic father* in the unconscious oedipal situation that involves a secondary identification with the castrating father.

This *symbolic father* must be distinguished from the *actual father's* ongoing and active developmental contribution throughout the child's life. Actual, flesh-and-blood fathers themselves have seldom been portrayed as real people, and their tangible impact has most often been studied only when there was paternal absence, neglect, abuse, or other overtly negative dynamics. Over the last half century, the impact of both the *flesh-and-blood father* and the *symbolic father,* as well as of the *paternal function* itself, has more likely been missing or lost (Diamond 1998, 2017a; Perelberg 2015).[1]

This is indeed unfortunate given what I believe to be a key point in considering male psychological development: that the boy's and later the man's *masculinity is greatly impacted* by the *actual* father (or surrogate) and his capacity to carry the *symbolic or paternal function* as the third in both the *attracting* and *separating* roles. In addition, as I will discuss later in the chapter, the father's *watchfully protective* functioning—in which autonomy and connection are synthesized—both reflects and contributes to a more developed sense of masculinity, for himself and for his son.

It remains controversial as to whether or not the actual father allies or misallies with his symbolic function and paternal representation—though as I mention later in this chapter, Lacan (2005) believed that the actual father is called upon to exercise this function through the father's "no" (*Non-du-Père*). However, in representing psychoanalytic structural thinking with its phylogenetic roots familiar to continental European and Latin American analysts, Perelberg (2015) argues that the symbolic father and paternal function refer to founding myths of psychoanalysis and culture. Hence, in reflecting a view that incorporates a more abstract level of conceptualization, symbolic functioning cannot be impacted by the father's actual presence. In challenging this perspective and drawing on developmental and clinical findings, many North American and Anglophone theorists argue that the father's actual presence or absence (as well as the mother's approbation of the father) influence the activation, development, and maintenance of symbolic and paternal functions (Diamond 2017a). Moreover, Freud (1900, 1921, 1930) never lost sight of the importance of the *actual* father's impact on the child's sense of reality (or, implicitly, of the *maturing intimacy* of the genital stage). For instance, he noted that the father's death is "the most important event ... [and] poignant loss of a man's life" (1900, p. xxvi), and, as I note later in this chapter, there is no greater need in childhood than the "need for a father's protection" (1930, p. 27).

The nature and strength of both the *internal father representation* and *symbolic functioning*—in which each remains potentially accessible if "awakened" or activated, perhaps through the analytic relationship (Eizirik 2015)—appreciably depend on the psychic maturation of the actual, involved father (or surrogate) in his relationship with the mother and child. In short, as I will argue in this chapter, this accomplishment hinges on the extent to which he has attained sufficient genital masculinity that integrates healthy phallicism with his relational needs. This paternal achievement entails a well-developed capacity for *responsibility for the other*—including *the other within the self* that, as discussed in Chapter 2, is often construed as feminine (Diamond 2020)—perhaps reflecting the father's adequate internalization of the maternal/feminine order originating in the mother-infant bond. In this respect, the active and penetrating qualities of the father's parenting—as well as the receptive and caregiving ones—become a foundation for his child's healthy gender identity and an important determinant of his child's psychic development.

This is particularly so for the boy child in that the relationship with his adult father sets the course for his subsequent male-to-male relationships.

Specifically, depending on the father's ability to reciprocate his son's homoerotic attachment to him, as well as on his capacity to manage his more phallic and oedipal impulses to shame his male child, the son is less likely to carry the sense of being unduly submissive, subordinate, inferior to, shamed by, or humiliated by other males (Chodorow 2012).

The idea of recovering the missing, abolished, and lost father, including his symbolic authority, has taken hold during more recent theorizing. As I will elaborate in Chapter 5, most children turn to their fathers (or surrogates)—either in actual or symbolic presence—in order to separate from intense wishes for and fears of fusional dependence on their mothers, often through fantasies of incorporating the father's phallic strength (Lacan 1993; McDougall 1989). Thus, the father as *the necessary third*—typically, but not always—protects the child, in both *actual* and *symbolic* functioning, from the perils arising from the absolute power held by the mother over the young child. At least, this is so in the child's unconscious perception that the mother's desires pose an existential threat of narcissistic collapse; the child may feel sucked into the powerful mother's "deadly embrace ... towards [indistinct] non-being" (Civitarese 2013, p. 125).

It should be noted that, as suggested in endnote 1, increasing evidence demonstrates that the paternal third is *not* necessarily the male-sexed father and, as will be discussed in Chapter 5, that triangularity in no way depends on the gendered presence of a father. Indeed, females, including the mother herself, often carry the paternal or symbolic function. For instance, single mothers can introduce the Law as a third element since "there are multiple third dimensions that cannot be reduced to the empirical presence of the 'father'" (Perelberg 2013, p. 581).

As I will discuss later in this chapter (in the section entitled "The symbolic 'third,' the paternal function, and French psychoanalysis: anchoring the separating role"), the symbolic order is primary in the form of the *Name of the Father*, the paternal metaphor or figure of Law that institutes the essential experience of (alienation and) separation from the maternal realm (Lacan 2005). The father blocks his child from living in the wished-for (and feared) merger with the mother—an imaginary world of omnipotent fantasy entailing ecstatic release without hindrance (*jouissance*). The *idea of the father* (i.e., the paternal function) imposes a Symbolic order that opens up three-dimensional space in which thought replaces action, which requires inhibition, loss, limits, and mourning.

Throughout the remainder of this chapter, and especially in the aforementioned later section, I will address in detail how the paternal function continues to remain a centerpiece of contemporary theory. In addition, I will clarify three main ways that today's conceptualizations of *the father* are taken up and the particular impact each has on the male's sense of his maleness: first, as an *actual, flesh-and-blood presence*, which manifests both in the boy's need for a father and in the subsequent challenges males face in fathering; second, as an *internal, intrapsychic representation* or imago; and finally, as *the third* in the mind's triadic, oedipal structure. Let's consider next the role played by the actual, flesh-and-blood father.

Boys and their fathers: homoerotic love and melancholic loss

The little boy's preoedipal, dyadic, father-son *homoerotic love* (Blos 1985; Diamond 1998)—his "typically masculine ... special interest in his father" that has nothing to do with "a passive or feminine attitude towards ... father (and ... males in general)" (Freud 1921, p. 105), comparable to the boy's heteroerotic desires for his mother—is inherently problematic because, just as in relation to his desires for mother, unconscious incestuous anxieties are generated, which in this case accelerate the repudiation of his homoerotic love for the father. Hence, in combination with cultural mores, as noted in Chapter 3 and subsequently considered in Chapter 6, the boy's same-sex object desire often tends to be preemptively foreclosed (Jay 2007). In addition, as further discussed in Chapter 5, the mother's unconscious attitude toward the child's father becomes crucial in determining the boy's ability to internalize the necessary triangular structure.

In revising disidentification theory, as discussed in Chapters 1 and 3, we find that the preoedipal, dyadic father is crucial in regulating the severity of his son's traumatic separation from his mother. We should keep in mind, however, that even if fathers are physically or emotionally unavailable, they are *always* psychically present and thereby able to represent the symbolic paternal function (Aisenstein 2015; Eizirik 2015). Paternal imagoes are created, even among fatherless children, who continue to represent two caretaking objects, one of whom serves to facilitate separating/individuating from the world of the other.

The young male's situation is made even more complex by the fact that, typically, boys do not grow up experiencing themselves as masculine by dint of being male, and thus, given its fragility, masculinity must be repeatedly proven, even in non-Westernized cultures (Gilmore 1990). This effort to establish a sufficiently secure sense of masculinity results in an ongoing predicament that remains unfathomable for many if not most men. Lacking the capacity to legitimate itself, masculinity "always needs affirmation .... no matter how complete [it] suspects itself of pretending" (Moss 2012, p. 7).

To reiterate, owing to the drive to individuate and the incest taboo, combined with culturally enforced aspects of his separation from the maternal orbit, the young boy often experiences his need for and identification with his mother as shameful, while also likely disavowing or foreclosing his active albeit receptive, typically masculine desire for his father (and the male sex in general). This is evident in adult males' defensive efforts against neediness to stave off shame states that are occasioned by penetration anxieties—often in receptive, passive, and/or sexualized countenance—that are equated with femininity.

We see this in the case of Brad, discussed in the previous chapter—specifically, in Brad's creation of narcissistic *psychic retreats* (Steiner 2011) and *impenetrable citadels* (Elise 2001) erected to fend off his essential incompleteness grounded in the complex relationship to his mother, hence preventing his being seen as vulnerable and lacking. Other examples of male shame are to be found in melancholic states of loss associated with disavowed homoerotic love when males join together in unacknowledged loving groups (typically, heterosexual ones), often sharing their internalized homophobia by repudiating the feminine.

Challenges to masculinity in becoming a father

Fatherhood marks a man's entrance both into the world of parenthood and into a more empathic appreciation of his own father's experience. This further establishes his sense of adult masculinity, replete with cultural and social expectations that tend to become salient as fatherhood approaches. Consequently, the process of fathering often triggers tremendous inner turmoil that, for some men, will interfere with becoming a father. For these men, issues pertaining to masculinity may be accompanied by defensive organizations that can promote more regressive, phallic-dominated defensive retreats.

For example, men who are dominated by narcissistically based forms of masculine striving, when initially called upon to father, may become depressed. Or more frequently, they may act out by having affairs, abandoning the family, losing themselves in work or addictive substance abuse, and generally becoming unavailable as watchful protectors—in a sort of paternal version of postpartum depression. The tragic quality of such failed fathering is compounded by the male's deepening sense of shame and guilt surrounding his arrested sense of manhood. The case of Rich, discussed later in this chapter, illustrates a man's struggles along these lines in initially embracing his fathering function.

An important challenge for the new father in coming to terms with his evolving more genital, less phallic form of masculinity (reflecting an attenuation of his need to legitimate his manhood) is to see his manhood as incorporating both the ability to stand alone and an increased capacity to connect by allowing the individuality of others to exist and thrive. This is evident in the statement of a patient, a former star athlete, who described his experience of containfully watching his wife interacting with their infant daughter:

> I watched them playing with each other and I knew that I would destroy something they were sharing if I made my presence known. It was difficult to just watch; I wanted to get in there and do something … maybe toss my daughter up in the air or tickle her. I resisted the temptation, though, and I am glad. That evening, I noticed I felt "older and heavier," not so "light and spry." But you know, I felt more like a man that night than I ever have, even before when I played football.

The instinctual basis of fathering

The more instinctual basis of fathering has been examined in the literature, despite the prevailing belief that fathers are further removed from the instinctual roots of parenting than are mothers. This psychogenetic approach to fathering has emphasized both the father's function as a provider and his capacity for fatherly ties, which render his relationship to his children a mutual, developmental experience (Diamond 1986, 2007).

Benedek (1970), for example, posited an instinctually rooted character trait termed *genuine fatherliness,* which enables a father to act toward his children with immediate empathic responsiveness. Indeed, there are latent predispositions for paternal caretaking, even among nonhuman species—for instance, male primates assist with birth, protect infants and their mothers from predators, and actively nurture the young to the point of becoming primary caretakers when necessary (Redican 1976). Such trends are observable among humans in the psychophysiological forms of father *engrossment* with the newborn (Greenberg and Morris 1974) and in father-infant *biorhythmic synchrony* (Pruett 1987). The genetic precursors to such fatherliness are described as *generativity* and *nurturance* (Ross 1975).

Nonetheless, the developmental forerunners of the father's capacity for *protectiveness*, particularly in its original *watchful* functions, have not been investigated. Consequently, what I describe as the father's *watchful protectiveness* (Diamond 1995), as I subsequently discuss in this chapter, helps create the conditions for a healthy mother-infant bond, particularly during the mother's primary maternal preoccupation (Winnicott 1965). In short, in addition to significant aspects of fatherly *protectiveness* that involve holding, containing, defending, and providing, *watchfulness* should be emphasized as an additional salient feature. This emphasis is warranted ontogenetically, as evident in its serving as the foundation for the other protective qualities just mentioned. Moreover, watchfulness develops throughout the mammalian species from an earlier precursor in the form of a built-in protective mechanism.

The process of becoming a father begins long before the child's conception and birth. Furthermore, the father's actual attachment and relationship to his infant—namely, the precursors to a generative, nurturing fatherliness—precede labor and delivery as well (Ross 1975, 1982). Just as the roots of a woman's motherhood are traceable to the distant past and the little girl's wishes to be like her mother and to actualize her maternal yearning to (re-)create through nurturance, so, too, can the foundations of a father's attachment and relationship to his infant be discerned in the little boy's procreative and defensive instincts, wishes, and behaviors, which are linked to his relationships to both mother and father.

Fathering as a maturational opportunity

Although fathers are increasingly involved in pregnancy, childbirth, and early parenting, as a culture, we have all too often neglected a full understanding of the positive and negative nuances of this experience for the father. For many men, the wife's (or partner's) pregnancy, along with subsequent facets of fathering, provides an occasion to move toward new and more satisfying resolution of sex and gender conflicts. In becoming a father and hopefully engaging in actual fathering, a man is given the opportunity to develop a more mature gender identity by renouncing and mourning his phallic wish to be unlimited, in the context of recognition and acceptance of certain real limits vis-à-vis sex and gender, as well as generational differences.

An examination of studies of adult men's experiences during the sequence of prospective fatherhood indicates that the emerging father must deal with and adequately master a number of emotional and psychological issues that become manifest during the course of this sequence in order to achieve the caregiving role of *genuine fatherliness* (Diamond 1986; Gurwitt 1976). Furthermore, there are many external sources of interference with a father's holding, protective functioning. Both socioeconomic factors and unforeseen trauma may create unfavorable birthing conditions. These external sources include naturally oc-curring disasters, physical illness or death, and severe psychological illness (particularly in the mother), as well as unavoidable work-related, financial, and/ or social-political conflicts, such as war or career circumstances requiring that the father be unavailable or removed from the family.[2]

Unconscious conflicts, as evident in this chapter's clinical account of Rich, may be triggered for a man while his wife is pregnant; for example, there may be envy of the prospective mother, concerns regarding responsibility for im-pregnation, anxieties about adulthood and aging, issues with competition and wishes to reestablish connection with one's own father, wishes to revitalize one's own parents, and jealousy and guilt toward the fetus who is the object of the partner's rapt attention. Given sufficient spousal and social support, however, most men are able to weather these difficulties sufficiently so that their fatherly instincts are not undercut. Indeed, the father's watchful holding of the mother-baby dyad can constructively serve to protect him from his destructive envy of motherhood and to compensate him for feeling unim-portant and left out of that dyad. This adaptively provides him with a sense of narcissistic fulfillment and completion along more neutralized phallic lines as "proof of … his masculine life-giving potency" (Manninen 1993, p. 38).

The fundamental psychological task for most men during this period involves the ubiquitous need for creative expression and subliminatory activity, in addition to containing and/or working through more neurotic conflicts as well as other forms of psychopathology. The man who can find constructive ways to express his fatherly ties during this challenging period, while simultaneously protecting his partner's (and child's) health and privacy by serving as a source of strength and support, emerges more fully with a healthy paternal identity while preparing for the long and winding road of fathering (Diamond 1998, 2007).

During the earlier stages on this road, initially with his newborn and then during his offspring's early childhood, the actual father (or surrogate) is called upon to fulfill two essential fathering functions that will remain important throughout the lives of both the father and his child: to serve as the *watchfully protective father*, and then to become the *attracting and separating father*. Let's consider next the first of these two functions.

The watchfully protective father

The archaic and universal wish to be tended to, protected, and provided for is experienced in both imaginary and actual relationships with others throughout the life span. The Christian paternal imagery of "Our Father which art in heaven" (Matthew 5:9-13) is the foremost Western depiction of this fundamental longing. As this imagery implies, the preeminent representation of such a protector and provider role is that of the father.

Freud (1930) stressed the gravity for the child of such paternal protectiveness when he stated: "I cannot think of any need in childhood as strong as the need for a father's protection" (p. 27). Children of fathers who were unable to provide sufficient *protective agency* during the earliest phases of their lives are less likely to receive important fatherly provisions at later stages, even though there are subsequent opportunities for reparative paternal contributions (Diamond 1998). This provision of protective agency early in children's lives is quite pressing, and its absence has wide-ranging social and psychological implications. There is evidence, for example, that children of fathers less involved in these initial phases of fathering are more likely during later childhood (and adult) development to incur paternal sexual abuse and the detrimental effects of uninvolved or ineffective fathering, including *father hunger* (Herzog 1982a), as well as (and in line with this book's focus) the more rigidly defensive organization of gender experience. Indeed, a father's *protective agency* function remains important throughout his child's development, though its forms will alter and its significance will recede as other fatherly provisions become more salient throughout the life cycle.

In accepting his traditional familial caregiving role, the father is provided with an important opportunity for overcoming developmental obstacles and working through intrapsychic conflicts (affecting gender identity, generativity, and mature object relations), while creating new familial legacies of male nurturance. Fathers capable of such engagement are more likely to experience an increased sense of familial worth and personal self-esteem as they become engrossed in the newborn child. Such fatherly provision additionally increases marital satisfaction, although the long-term effects remain unknown (Pruett 1993).

The selfless generosity, sacrifice, and servitude required by such early forms of fathering strengthen a man's sense of "real" manhood, primarily because such fatherly protection and provision serve the imperatives of a man's ego ideal as determined by his unique development, while simultaneously fulfilling his culture's *ubiquitous code of masculinity* (Gilmore 1990). The attainment of this life step (among other developmental passages) indicates the maturing male's mastery and integration of his phallic urges into their more aim-inhibited forms.

This more developed form of masculinity required of the watchfully protective father synthesizes autonomy and connection. The aptitude for paternal watchfulness, the *protective fathering function*, is partly an outcome of the new father's own earliest maternal and paternal identifications. Moreover, his ability to provide such protective watchfulness depends on his capacity for more vicarious, less direct forms of gratification through identification and empathic object relationships (Diamond 1998, 2007).

The ability to succeed in functioning as a watchfully protective father partly depends on the degree to which he can deal appropriately with his envy of intense mother-infant mutuality. An initial jealousy of the mother-infant bond is natural, after all, but the *protectively holding* father must successfully integrate both the creative and destructive aspects of his envy. This synthesis results both from his creative expression, which further establishes his tie to the infant, and from his identification with the blissful union experienced by mother and baby. Moreover, the mother's sensitivity to the father's needs and her attunement to her husband's feelings of loss can help ameliorate his sense of exclusion and rivalry.

The act of watchfully protecting enables the father to reexperience both his attachment to and loss of his own early paternal object, while simultaneously accessing and reworking his disavowed maternal identifications. The boy's unique developmental dilemma of how he is to become a male while maintaining a close connection with his mother is re-created for the man when called upon to watchfully protect his progeny. Like the growing boy who learns to join his needs for autonomy with his needs for connection, the father who becomes engrossed in his newborn while "holding" the mother-infant dyad is able to simultaneously experience a *loving union with the world* and to acknowledge the *fact of its otherness* (Chasseguet-Smirgel 1985). The father's watchful protectiveness of the mother-infant dyad enables him to connect directly with the world lying beyond his control, while further attenuating his own infantile omnipotence through what might be understood as an *optimal disillusionment*.

In serving as the original protective agent for the mother-infant dyad, the father also shields the mother from impingement and interference from without while she carries, bears, and suckles their infant. Thus, particularly before the infant can make use of him in other ways, the watchful father frees the mother to devote herself to their baby. As noted earlier, in holding the mother-infant dyad near the end of pregnancy and for several weeks after the baby's birth, the father is able to promote the mother's necessary *primary maternal preoccupation* (Winnicott 1956), which becomes the basis for the infant's ego establishment. Thus, as a delegate of the outside world in his *husbandry* function, the father provides for and serves as an external beacon to his wife and child, protecting their intense, primary mutuality with one another.

In short, the attuned, watchfully protective father is especially able to "parent his wife" at the very time she most needs such care (Herzog 1982b). By adaptively elevating his infant (along with the mother-infant bond) by projecting his ego ideal onto the infant, he is more able to treat the baby (and the mother-infant dyad) as complete. Consequently, through unconsciously accessing his own primordial vulnerability—namely, the *prephallic* facet of his maleness—the father's longing for the primitive sense of fusion manifests principally as an attachment to his infant as a differentiated object.

Furthermore, the involved father who is able to watch over, hold, and protect the mother and the developing fetus, infant, and small child is likely in due course to become the father who must again hold, bear, and support with interested restraint his adolescent child's identity experimentation and subsequent distancing from family dependencies. As I discuss further in Chapter 5, through the father's functioning in this way, typically in conjunction with a sufficiently attuned mother able to recognize her son's masculinity, the severity of what might be potentially traumatizing for the little boy who is engaged in the separation-individuation process is mitigated.

In serving as the earliest representative of the *nonmother* world (Abelin 1975), the actual father or surrogate in his *attracting/separating function*—namely, the *functional agent of separation* (Harris 2008; see also Kristeva 2014)—comes to represent *difference* and invariably carries a paternal quality as *third* (Green 1986, 2004). As I've noted, this representation as third may occur even in circumstances when the second parent is neither the biological father nor even male. Regardless, these fundamental qualities of fathering—nurturing, protecting, and holding, as well as subsequently attracting and separating the son from the mother's world—reflect and require a more flexible sense of masculinity that facilitates consolidating the boy's integration of his maternal-feminine identifications.

In addition, through his providing function, the new, albeit more traditional father often "feathers the nest" by working diligently to gain greater income or career status in order to look after his wife and "young fledgling" (Pollack 1995). In his empathic responsiveness to his child's dyadic needs, the new father guards and gives sanctuary to the particulars of maternal biological contact and feeding. The progressive developmental accomplishments that depend upon this early fathering contribution increase the chances that even in a grown child's mid- to late adulthood, a healthy internal sense of being watched over will remain vibrantly alive.

This connection with a "good" internal father originates while the father remains outside his child's earliest dyadic attachment, prior to the child's preoedipal triangulation with the parents. This in no way implies, however, that fathers do not experience their own unique dyadic bonding with their children.

The mutual bonds experienced by fathers with their sons and daughters are powerfully rewarding and extremely important in each one's interactive development (Blos 1985; Diamond 1998). My point is that this initial paternal function of *protective agency* operates largely outside these dyadic bonds. Moreover, for the adult—the child who has grown up—the universal longing for protection and watchfulness by a caring other is boldly revealed in George Gershwin and Ira Gershwin's (1926) captivating jazz-era lyrics:

> There's a somebody I'm longing to see
> I hope that he turns out to be
> Someone who'll watch over me ....
> Oh! How I need, someone to watch over me.
> —"Someone to Watch Over Me" (from *Oh, Kay*)
> by George and Ira Gershwin

Fathers who succeed in providing these functions seem better able to connect with their inner lives while maintaining a valuation of the outside world beyond mother-child primary mutuality (Diamond 1986). The *alliance of pregnancy*, characterized by the husband's empathy with his spouse, subsequently evolves at delivery into a sense of the "whole becoming greater than the sum of its parts," while a "feeling of awe" tends to accompany an emerging sense of family and parenting alliance (Herzog 1982b).

The genital father's role in establishing triangular space: inhabiting the attracting and separating paternal functions

The boy's ability to internalize this healthy *genital father* imago depends on, among other factors, the nature of the father's relationship with the mother, and hers with the father. As well, a genital father (who is able to embody his son's ego ideal) can be internalized only when a *real*, flesh-and-blood other has already provided the "good enough" fathering that typically can be observed initially in the mutual involvement of the early, dyadic father-son relationship and later in reciprocal identifications throughout the oedipal phase (Diamond 1998, 2007).

This genital father effectively embodies the Law of the Father that includes the elements of absence, lack, and loss in pointing to something inherently unattainable (Lacan 1949, 1953, 2005); yet, through inhabiting the *attracting* fathering function, he offers child and spouse a dyadic relationship with him that is both parallel to and competes with the mother-son unit. As I will discuss further in Chapter 5, sons with coupled parents jointly regarding their child are more oriented toward the psyche's essential thirdness and are better able to represent the self in triadic relationship. This sets the course for a more favorable oedipal phase and healthy gender identity development. When deficient, the boy's representation of himself becomes problematic—as seen in the shame-based, obsessive, and perverse defensive configurations evident in a very tenuous sense of masculinity shorn of triangular space. We saw this in the case of Brad, discussed in the previous chapter, and will see it again in the cases of Charles and Jake, described in Chapter 5.

A father is frequently called upon to invite his wife to return to their conjugal relationship so that she learns to divide her focus between the maternal and spousal parts of herself. The mother may need her husband to maintain the sexual component of "spousing and caregiving," particularly in the face of her wishes that her husband remain "the nonsexual man who can entertain the child" (Herzog 2005b, p. 66). By drawing his wife back to him in the context of his engaged fathering, the father protects the marriage's adult sexuality and intimacy while facilitating his son's efforts to differentiate from his primary object. Through firm yet sensitive efforts to restore the couple's suspended sexuality, the father, in his genital countenance, uses his erotic manliness to strengthen his connection with his wife and to provide his son an object of identification able to locate maleness within the matrix of intimate relationship. This sexual bond between parents provides the child with "a rock to which he can cling and against which he can kick" (Winnicott 1964, p. 115).

In this fashion (which I will address further in Chapter 5), a father helps his son recognize the link joining his parents together and thereby establishes *triangular space* (Britton 1989). By being both a caring father to his son and an exciting lover to his wife, he offers each a dyadic relationship with him that is parallel to and competes with the mother-son dyad. In reclaiming his wife and son, the relating man—having integrated his phallic propensities with his genital aims—supplies a vital anchor for both his child and his partner. Accordingly, the boy is better able to represent himself with his mother, his father, and with mother and father together. When the boy is jointly regarded by his parents rather than individually appropriated by either for their unconscious need fulfillment, the oedipal phase is successfully achieved, with preoedipal triadic reality having functioned as its prerequisite (Herzog 2005a).

In contrast, when the father is unable to join with his wife to facilitate his son's internalization of triadic reality, the boy's identification with his mother becomes problematic and negatively affects his masculine gender identity. This is evident in some boys' more hysterical and perverse reactions to the prospect of separating from the mother; disavowing their own and the mother's sexuality, they unconsciously remain in the position of the little boy with his presexual mother. These boys, such as Charles (discussed in the next chapter), manifest profoundly shame-based defensive configurations that reflect a tenuous sense of masculinity.

Every boy is born into a triangular structure that precedes him, and he will form his identifications in the context of that structure (Perelberg 2013). Consequently, internalizing a genital father imago—whereby the father has sufficiently neutralized his phallic masculinity to care for an *other*—also depends on the nature of the actual father's relationship to the mother and hers with the father. As I've indicated, this results largely from the fact that, as we are reminded by some of the continental European and Latin American analysts who are anchored in structural thinking (Aisenstein 2015; Eizirik 2015), the father is an ever-present *third* in the triangular form of the mother-child and father-child unconscious linkages.

As noted in previous chapters, it is well recognized that a crucial role in the child's developing identity is played by unconscious interpsychic communication, particularly the unconscious wishes and enigmatic inscriptions of gender assignment between the parents, as well as between parent and child (Laplanche 1997, 2007). Although this domain of the unconscious relations of parents to their children "has ultimately been very poorly explored" (ibid. 2007, p. 215), the primacy of triadic interactions—the infant's *triangular competence*—has been extensively studied by researchers, who have demonstrated that an infant engaged with either parent spontaneously looks to the other in order to bring the missing one into the encounter (Fivaz-Depeursinge and Corboz-Warnevy 1999; Fivaz-Depeursinge, Lavanchy-Scaiola, and Favez 2010).

Though my focus here and in Chapter 5 is primarily on traditional heterosexual coupling, triadic parenting issues also pertain to homosexual couples—in addition to single parents for whom the *third* is delegated to a surrogate or agent of the symbolic function, in which the adult representing the *second other* is called upon to draw the primary nurturer back into their sexual liaison. Both partners' identifications with their own feminine and masculine caregivers play a significant role, as evident in my discussion of the father's presence in the mother's mind and vice versa. Moreover, this *second other* or *third* (to the mother-child dyad), ideally in a *genital paternal* countenance, is equally important to the development of both the gay boy and the straight boy; it helps determine the child's relationship to his masculine gender identity—namely, his sense of maleness in being gay, bisexual, or straight. Here it is useful to note the unique yet overlapping developmental trajectories of homosexual and heterosexual boys, although the pathways along which the homosexual child begins to experience homoerotic attraction are more complicated, requiring the father's affirmation of his son's masculine identity as an "outsider" (Frommer 1994; see also Isay 1989; Lewes 1988).

The involved father

Freud (1921) first observed that the father plays an important role in the establishment of his son's gender identity within the early triadic relationship. He later (1925) wrote of the boy's early love for his father and the ubiquity of psychic bisexuality. To extend these Freudian observations, as described in Chapters 1 and 3 and elaborated later in this chapter, in the little boy's turning away from his mother and experiencing loss, an available preoedipal father tempers his son's defensive tendency to disengage forcefully from her (Diamond 2004b). Furthermore, abundant evidence now exists demonstrating specific contributions that involved fathers make to their children's development (summarized in Diamond 2007).[3]

Unlike both Seth and Brad, the patients discussed in Chapters 2 and 3, respectively, each of whom lacked a preoedipal, sufficiently genital father who might have helped his son from being exceedingly vulnerable to feeling shamed by other males, the boy who is able to achieve a *reciprocal identification* with an available, loving father who possesses a body and genitalia like his own—who is like the boy but who remains independent and outside the boy's control—is provided with a foundation for a more secure (and often more varied) gendered expression of the self. As is particularly apparent in the analyst's occupying this position with Seth—given his real father's failings—this affirming, mutual bond with the father (or his surrogate) facilitates the son's integration of maternal feminine identifications, as well as helping him overcome the "fault lines" of being easily humiliated in relation to other males (Chodorow 2012).

When there is a marked absence of sufficient fathering—particularly in its attracting and separating paternal functioning—the analytic process itself (and the analyst) can provide an opportunity for the necessary *identifications with* and *by* the father (or father-analyst) to be "activated/reactivated through the analytic relationship" (Eizirik 2015, p. 344). We can see that these identifications allow the *active and penetrating* as well as the *receptive and caregiving* qualities of the fathering function to become a foundation for healthier gender identity, as evident with Seth (Chapter 2) and Jake (Chapter 5). This reciprocal bond has been aptly termed *mutual recognition* (Benjamin 1988), which is pivotal in a father's facilitation of his son's development beyond the phallic-narcissistic position in staving off shame states (Chodorow 2012; Diamond 2007; Kaftal 1991).

Let's turn next to the challenge that the father often faces in fulfilling his separating function.

As considered in the previous two chapters, then, at around age three, even as they turn toward the world of the father, boys face another loss in relation to the mother. They begin to experience her in a new way, in a sexual manner, in addition to her accustomed role as maternal nurturer. Preoedipal splitting occurs and the boy feels he has two mothers (and two selves)—one that is *pregenital* and one that is *genital*. Conflict then emerges as to which mother he desires, the *evocative sexual* one or the *comforting nurturer*, and temporary refuge from this conflict is sought. A way to achieve this is by putting the conflict outside the mother-child relation, setting up the father as *the second other* (Greenspan 1982) and thus the one to blame.

As a result of occupying the *symbolic father function* and thereby standing for sexuality in the boy's unconscious, the father is blamed for breaking the bliss of ignorance and turning it into the sin of sexual knowledge. The father is consequently called on to accept this potentially adaptive projection and to bear his child's hatred toward the outside-the-mother world that fathers represent. However, when the father fails to metabolize this projection and provide a healthy preoedipal genital object for identification, the little boy, in a "hysterical" effort to resolve his conflict, seeks a return to the mother through desexualizing both the self and the mother (Bollas 2000). Lacking a father who can assume a sufficient paternal function, the little boy tends to idealize his mother's nonsexual characteristics and turns her into a Madonna mother and the self into a sexual innocent as "a perfect little boy" (ibid.). In short, then, without the father's containing and involved, attracting/separating genital presence to keep the boy linked in his mind both to mother and to father, an opposition can form between love and sexuality that encourages the boy's view of sexuality as a form of separation from maternal-like love. This is often the precursor to the *Madonna/whore* complex, illustrated in the case of Charles (Chapter 5).

In the course of the boy's relationship with a father (or father surrogate) whom he admires and who interacts with and mentors him in a caring (rather than shaming) way, in part through bearing such projections, the boy is able to internalize a paternal imago in which the *active and penetrating* aspects and the *receptive and caregiving* qualities of the father's parenting become a foundation for healthy and fluid masculine gender identity. This fathering imago reflects both the attracting and separating facets of healthy paternal functioning—namely, *genital fathering*. In other words, a father who represents genital masculinity, whose adaptive phallic strivings are integrated with his more relationally oriented, connected, and nurturing masculine qualities, helps set the stage for his son's healthy sense of maleness—one in which a fragile masculinity no longer requires rigid defending by warding off either the fearfully feminine or the terrifying shame of being humiliated by other boys (and later, men).[4]

It is striking that the nurturing and protective qualities of this earliest father contradict the more universal, *phallic gender* stereotype of men as active, penetrating, and potent (Diamond 1997). These fundamental genital qualities of fathering reflect a more flexible sense of masculinity and thus can facilitate the integration of the boy's maternal-feminine identifications through the internalization of a relationship with an admired man who interacts in ways other than a phallic manner. Moreover, as noted earlier in this chapter, the father-son homoerotic attraction is often more complicated for the gay child (or gay father) and may require the father's affirmation of his son's sense of maleness as an admirable and loved *outsider*.

Indeed, certain parental roles, such as providing an ego-supportive *holding environment* (Winnicott 1956), serving as a steady and responsive *container* for a baby's unpleasant feelings (Bion 1959), and supplying *empathic mirroring* (Kohut 1971), have been historically conceived as *maternal* in function. It is not surprising, therefore, that the more receptive and serene paternal functions involving holding, containing, waiting, and empathy have long been ignored, presupposed as maternal or feminine traits, or simply treated as insignificant and peripheral. Especially for men whose psyches are organized around the phallic position, yielding to these faculties can provide an opportunity to challenge the need to repudiate their putative femininity.

The symbolic "third," the paternal function, and French psychoanalysis: anchoring the separating role

As noted at the beginning of this chapter, the father's vital role is established initially within the early triadic relationship through the *symbolic father function* that cuts the symbiotic, regressive tie to the archaic mother, promotes shifting from an *imaginary* relationship with the mother, and encourages separateness (Freud 1913, 1921, 1923, 1939; see also Loewald 1951; McDougall 1989). Both Freud and Lacan viewed identification with the symbolic father as a *function* that was established prior to the cathexis of the mother, and the symbolic father is understood to be quite distinct from the father as a "real," embodied person.

For Lacan, in his extension of Freud's ideas, the Symbolic order becomes primary through the Name of the Father or *Nom-du-Père* (Lacan 1949, 1953, 2005); consequently, language as an internal possession aids the child in differentiating his/her body from the mother's body. The *symbolic father* as a function (concentrating in itself both *imaginary* and *real* relations) establishes the necessary internal representation signifying the Law and representing reality by standing in the way of primal fusion. This blocks the child from an imaginary world of omnipotent fantasy entailing ecstatic release without hindrance (*jouissance*). Therefore, in order for thought to exist, integration of the father as the paternal function is essential; accordingly, when this is foreclosed, psychosis can ensue because movement from the symbiotic maternal tie to the symbolic order cannot proceed (Lacan 1953).

Lacan proposed that—much as I argue in this chapter, and despite the fact that the symbolic father function is hidden and is *not* reducible to the embodied, sensual realm (Freud 1939)—the symbolic order is rendered primary through the *actual father's* exercise of this particular *separating* function, evident in the father's "no" (*Non-du-Père*—cf. Lacan 1949, 2005). Serving as the object of the mother's desire, and through being represented as the *third* element that breaks apart the collusion between mother and child, the father in his symbolic function separates mother and child by laying down the incest taboo. In short, in representing the symbolic basis of separation and renunciation—serving as a sort of symbolic castration—the *castrating* (*separating*) father opens up three-dimensional space wherein thought replaces action, which requires inhibition, loss, limits, lack, and mourning. Freud (1939) viewed this achievement as "a victory of *intellectuality over sensuality*" (p. 113, italics added).

Post-Lacanian Francophones, particularly Green (1986, 2004, 2009), McDougall (1989), and Laplanche (1989, 1997, 2007), elaborated the paternal function by focusing on the father's essential presence as the *third* in the mother's mind, necessary to preclude entrapment in a dual relationship. Hence, maturing masculinity is understood to emerge from the introduction of this third element that includes the subject, object, and other of the object in the mother's mind, particularly when augmented by the actual father's role as an agent of separation—decreeing prohibitions and offering himself as an object for identification, furthering healthy superego development.

Theoreticians writing in the French analytic tradition, in line with Freudian and post-Freudian theorists, address the father's place vis-à-vis the primary mother-child dual relationship. Though less developmentally or-iented than their counterparts in the English-speaking realm—including Peter Blos (1985), James Herzog (2004), John Munder Ross (1977), and me (Diamond 1998), each of whom has focused largely on the actual father's impact upon his preoedipal, oedipal, and postoedipal child—such French psychoanalysts as Lacan, Laplanche, Braunschweig and Fain, Chasseguet-Smirgel, McDougall, Green, and Aisenstein have played a major role in illuminating the father function. Arguably, they have also been highly in-fluential in recognizing the father as a primary object differentiated from the mother—that is, using my terminology, an internalized *genital father* that serves to stimulate processes of creation, symbolization, and sublimation.

In sum, as noted earlier in this chapter, the paternal function remains a centerpiece of classical and contemporary theory and is understood to reflect a complex interaction between the father's *actual presence, symbolic func-tioning*, and *internal representation* in both the child's mind and the mother's mind. In short, the father serves as (1) a significant figure in his child's development (a real, external object); (2) a fundamental internal object or intrapsychic representation (internal father); and (3) a central figure in the mind's basic triadic and oedipal structure (a structuralizing third).

Inhabiting the paternal function

Fathers, then, inhabit numerous positions, from castrators and separators to protectors, seducers, attractors, and affirmers. Before turning to a case that illustrates the importance of inhabiting, perhaps, the key fathering provision in assuming fatherhood, let's first briefly return to considering the father's important *separating function*, both in its actual flesh-and-blood form and its symbolic form.

As discussed in the preceding chapters, the boy's turning toward his father helps serve as a differentiating factor—a "fortress that keeps the mother out" (Glasser 1985, p. 409)—as the father comes to represent an alternative libidinal object to be internalized. Consequently, an available preoedipal father as the *second other* (Greenspan 1982) tempers the little boy's more defensive tendencies to disengage forcefully from his mother, while providing a conventional focus for masculine identification (Diamond 1998, 2004b).

Progressive differentiation, consequently, can predominate, rather than *opposition* in "disidentifying" from mother or repudiating feminine identifications. The presence of the father, both as a symbolic and an actual attracting, devoted, and attentive third, helps the boy differentiate and separate from his mother, his primary external object. His particular experience of loss actually facilitates his internalization of key aspects of his relationship with his mother. However, this is *not* the same as disidentifying from his *internal* maternal object because early identifications—especially primary identifications with the mother—are never simply removed or repudiated in the unconscious once and for all. Rather, the boy's early identifications with his mother and father remain significant in his psychic structure; typically, they become more accessible—and thus subject to mutative influences—as he matures.

Many men, however, struggle considerably with embracing the fathering function, and psychoanalytic help may be of significant value. The following case description suggests the kinds of conflicts that may arise partly as a consequence of a man's having lacked sufficient actual and symbolic fathering; these conflicts interfere with his acceptance of the watchfully protective function and engagement in an early preoedipal, dyadic relationship with his son.

The case of Rich: implications for fathering and masculinity[5]

Rich entered treatment at the age of thirty-four, shortly after his wife became pregnant. He felt "particularly depleted" by the excessive pressure of running his own business. Although quite successful, Rich felt driven to add extra accounts in order to "prepare for all the rainy days that lie ahead."

Early in therapy, he often spoke concerning his considerable misgivings about having a child. He explained, however, that he needed to accede to the desires of his 38-year-old wife, Nancy, since "her biological clock is running short and she's a 'natural mother.'"

Following his son Daniel's birth, Rich became more agitated and depressed and arranged for increased traveling and other activities that kept him busy outside the home. Despite having fathered the son that he "had always wanted," Rich nonetheless felt terrible about himself "as a man." As he explained, things had become more and more unpleasant at home because Nancy, when not exhausted, "always seems busy with our infant." Rich complained vehemently about her "devotion" to Daniel, and he angrily deplored her "lack of interest either in me or in sex."

By the time Daniel was about eight months old, Rich was well into his second year of analysis. Nancy had become increasingly enraged with him over his absences from the family and continued unavailability. She resented his constant neediness and demands while being so unable to give of himself. Rich struggled with how ashamed and cowardly he felt about his withdrawal. He realized that he was repeating his own father's pattern, which he recalled as leaving him all alone "in the hands of my crazy mother, who poked me incessantly." "Thank God that Nancy's not crazy," he added, "but still I can't stand watching her give so much love to Daniel while I feel so unloved and devalued."

In exploring his shameful withdrawal, Rich realized that he had made Nancy into an ideal version of his mother. He concurrently had re-created the sense of being left alone *without* a father's watchful protection (i.e., without an adequate dyadic, paternal identification that could serve as the forerunner to his projecting his ego ideal onto his *genital father*). Lacking an internal *watchful paternal presence*, Rich could not safely be alone without the idealized mother ("breast") he had made Nancy into and desperately clung to.

Rich could experience himself as a "whole man" only when he was able to relive the illusion of completely satisfying his own mother and could consequently reexperience himself as having recovered the "lost paradise" of being inside her. He stated, "I was Nancy's only man for so long, and she was so there for me." "It hurts to admit it," he continued, "but I don't want to share her because she'll just replace me with Daniel and I'll be all alone again." The "rainy days" that Rich had been compulsively preparing for could be understood as reflecting his infantile anxieties of being "left out in the cold"—a "cold" that rendered him feeling unprotected and in-adequately provided for, as if violently torn away from the warmth and comfort of a forever shattered human connection.

We were analyzing how his sense of masculinity and accompanying self-esteem were linked to his fantasy of having his wife all to himself, and in turn, his experience of her as the source of his longed-for return to an ideal state of happiness. Rich become more able to recognize, disclose, and bear his deep sense of shame and abandonment in his analysis as his experiences were connected to his *phallic ideals* born out of childhood grandiosity.

In one aspect of Rich's transference to me, I represented a *genital father* (able to both impregnate and provide) onto whom he could project his ego ideal. As we analyzed the conditions that caused him to experience himself as lacking such an internal genital father imago, he increasingly became able to access this paternal representation, while both projecting his archaic ego ideal onto his son and identifying simultaneously with Daniel as a self-extension in need of protective, involved fathering. A new internalization was evident, and Rich was well on his way toward developing a mature, healthier form of recognizing his son's *otherness*, which was facilitated by his beginning to see himself more frequently in little Daniel while accepting his own caregiving role as a father.

As a result of Rich's expanding psychic flexibility and ability to calm his earlier inner conflicts, his need to withdraw from Daniel and Nancy lessened, and he began to identify with Daniel as a self-extension in need of protective, involved fathering. Rich recognized how much his son needed a father who could be "the umbrella for Danny and his mother." He mused about how Daniel would need him in the years ahead, while genuinely appreciating Nancy's capacity to give so much love to their son.

In a session just after Daniel's first birthday, Rich proudly described the deepening father-son bond while noting his own increased acceptance of his differentiation from Nancy. He next turned his thoughts toward his relationship with his wife and observed that he was no longer draining her with his own neediness. He stated somewhat delightedly, "You know, now that Nancy isn't so tired all the time, I can even imagine her lusting after me again." Rich then playfully indicated both his steadily increasing differentiation from and connection to Nancy when he added the punch line: "But you know what? I just might not be in the mood myself!"

Brief case discussion

This case illustrates how a new father's conflicts and inhibited capacity to achieve watchful protectiveness, resulting partly from the absence of sufficient paternal functioning on his own father's part, can prevent him from fully assuming his fatherly (and husbandry) functions. However, once achieved, in this case through the analytic process, such fathering helps provide a good foundation for his infant child as well as a parenting alliance with his spouse, while strengthening his own emerging paternal identity and his more genital, adult sense of masculinity. The nature of a father's protective agency, his serving as the "someone watching over" from the outside, is multidetermined and based largely on the unique needs of his child, his wife, himself, and the operative marital, familial, and cultural system.

In ultimately being able to provide such watchful protection to his progeny, Rich himself reaped benefits in several ways, not the least of which was the opportunity he was given to reconstruct his own fundamentally conflicted, quite vulnerable sense of masculinity in a more cohesive and yet more flexible way. The quiet servitude inherent in this fundamental fatherly provision furnishes compelling evidence of the ability to repair and heal the earliest of male wounds by allowing the new father to create a unique and complex, maturing, and better integrated gender identity of his own.

Notes

1 The term *paternal function* is an unfortunate heir to the *paterfamiliae* of Roman law, apparently. The term seems to be based, arguably, on a power-dominated, hierarchical division of the sexes that essentializes a historical construction. A large number of third dimensions exist, and caretakers of either gender perform both maternal and paternal functions (Perelberg 2013). Contemporary analysts suggest using a nongendered term instead, such as *symbolic, triadic, not-mother,* or *third-party function* to denote the task of separating the child from the mother

in order to permit entry into a symbolic universe (Davies and Eagle 2013; Glocer Fiorini 2013). This deconstruction of the term foretells a movement beyond impoverishing dichotomies and *phallic logic* as gender-based parenting functions continue to shift, often radically (as subsequently noted in this chapter).

2 For instance, extraordinary demands are placed on fathers during adverse birthing situations involving high-risk pregnancies and/or premature or otherwise high-risk infants. Almost any father's capacity for protective watchfulness is severely compromised during these circumstances, which inevitably involve increased financial burdens and overwhelming needs to provide solid emotional support for a high-risk pregnant wife or new mother, in addition to an at-risk fetus or infant. These fathers must also confront emotionally demanding blows to their self-esteem, painful issues arising from feelings of helplessness, and grief pertaining to potential loss, while at the same time being forced to abdicate their paternal holding functions to physicians and nurses or other authorities.

3 For example, both Benjamin (1988, 1991) and Ross (1990) address the important role played by involved fathers with their daughters in particular, especially during prelatency phases. Pruett (1987, 1993) emphasizes that actively involved, nurturing fathers are uniquely important during the child's (whether male or female) earliest and later years, while numerous analytic writers have pointed out the relationship between the absence of such active, involved fathering and the many social and familial ills that plague societies (Herzog 1982a; Lansky 1992; Mitscherlich 1969).

4 A problematic legacy of classical Freudian oedipal theory is a tendency by some analysts to discuss the son's desire for his father primarily in *negative oedipal* terms—specifically, as the "negative" or "inverted" oedipal constellation. This is a regrettable interpretation of Freud, who wrote of the boy's early love for his father and the ubiquity of psychic bisexuality; the case of Seth, discussed in Chapter 2, could be seen as an example of this, given the patient's homoerotic identificatory love for me as his analyst-father. However, several post-Freudian analysts have incisively conceptualized the dyadic, early father-son relationship and the triangular dynamics of the rapprochement phase wherein both parents need to contain and manage their own separation issues and competitive, envious feelings (Abelin 1971, 1975; Blos 1985).

5 The case of Rich was previously discussed elsewhere (Diamond 1997, 2007).

5 The impact of mother and mother-with-father together

The key role of the mother in her son's developing gender identity, as well as the mother coupled with the father as her parenting partner, is explored in this chapter. The little boy's ultimate need to differentiate himself from his mother along gender lines—she being the originary as well as primary caregiver, typically—opens a developmental path for him that is quite distinct from that of the little girl. I examine ways in which the mother, either as a couple member or as a single parent, can foster or hinder her son's healthy gender identity development, depending especially upon her unconscious attitudes toward his maleness. After highlighting the clinical importance of the fundamental triad (the couple plus the child) evident in a parenting style that incorporates mother-and-father together, I present two clinical vignettes that illustrate the effects of a mother and father's failed triangular functioning; the result in both cases was a collusive mother-son dyad with a particular impact on the son.

The paradoxical relationship with the omnipotent mother

No mother (or father) can avert the child's primordial vulnerability resulting from the state of radical helplessness in which the dependent infant must receive everything from the mother who nurses his basic needs. As I discussed in my earlier chapters, this asymmetrical dependency on the first woman and seductress in every man's life leaves an unconscious residue of primordial vulnerability and discord—perhaps due to the human infant's distinctive prematurity at birth.

Though it remains a controversial concept, *primal repression* describes an archaic defense against the earliest impressions producing unnamable anxieties that are not registered at the time and cannot be recalled later in life (Freud 1900). The infant's radical helplessness is maintained and signified in an archaic mode—namely, in its original fragmented, iconic, and preverbal form that remains largely unrepresented, while preventing further semiotic development (Salomonsson 2014). Current understanding of such preverbal representation, as well as of the overinclusiveness of early mental representation (Fast 1990; Stern 1985), indicates that the relationship to separate objects begins with the nursing relationship. The basic elements of so-called psychic bisexuality—namely, being penetrated and penetrating—are contained in the infant's relationship to the nursing breast. Consequently, as I will expand upon, little boys rely on developing a gender split to defend against the omnipotent, penetrating breast-mother who presumably, as Kleinians propose, is dangerous because she is needed and envied (Elise 1996).

As I suggest (and research corroborates, as noted in Chapter 6), the infantile nursing situation produces a particularly terrifying charge for the infant male, who must rely on maternal regulatory functioning to an even greater extent than the female infant. When the distressed infant's originary anxieties cannot be contained and made tolerable (by the environmental mother), these terrors return in the form of *nameless dread* (Bion 1962), which may require the attacked yet fragile psyche to resort to drastic, autistic-like protective maneuvers (Tustin 1987) that, for some males, will subsequently manifest in rigid, impenetrable forms of phallicity.

The archaic mother reigning over the small boy becomes represented as the powerful, omnipotent figure whom he must be able to count on. The omnipotent mother imago, however, is also terrifying as a result of its association with his infantile helplessness, dependency, and projected hostility—particularly when he begins to separate and subsequently during the phallic stage when the horror (*abscheu*) of genital differences and castration anxiety become conscious. Partly to cope with the oral-based dangers of being annihilated by his engulfing, omnipotent mother in the context of longing for the satiety and security attained through fusion with her, he may develop the primal fantasy of abandoning himself in order to return to his mother's womb (Cournut 1998).

By means of deferred action (*après-coup*), the boy's terror of being completely possessed and thereby annihilated is further concretized. What has been described as the male's normative *core complex* (Glasser 1985) reflects this irreconcilable conflict produced by his longing for the primal mother as the only object able to gratify all his (infant) needs in the context of his simultaneous terror of being invaded, taken over, and mutilated (castrated) by her. The desire to free himself from his formidable mother, apparent in the Genesis myth, expresses his "victory ... over his mother and over women" (Chasseguet-Smirgel 1964, p. 133).

Because the first other is always a woman, the discordance is rendered more problematic for the boy than for the girl. For a girl and her mother, the separation process takes place within a relational matrix of bodily similarity that favors both representability and primary identification. In contrast, the paradox of the mother-son relationship lies in the fact that the closest and indispensable primary other is fundamentally different (i.e., lacking in the same sexual organs).

Freud's pithy adage questioning "what does a woman want?" (1925, p. 244) probably conveys the male's ever-present difficulty with understanding the maternally based, erotic feminine. Moreover, because the object that he loses throughout his earliest months is always *different from* rather than *similar to,* maternity is rendered all the more unrepresentable in its mysterious distinctiveness, and accordingly, the son is forever unable to understand his mother's maternal feminine dimension, while subsequently experiencing her erotic femininity as a betrayal. In contrast, the girl's similarity to mother offers her a greater opportunity for retrieving something of the relationship with her lost primary object, including the mother's own unconscious link—that is, in the Freudian lexicon of mourning (and melancholia), *the shadow*—of her lost primary maternal object. Boys, then, are forced to psychically work on—often through *après-coup*—both the distresses and the excitations caused by an inescapable acknowledgment of these differences (Bollas 2000; Cournut 1998; David 1973).

As I elaborated in Chapter 4, the boy's need to turn to his father as an alternative object with whom he can achieve a bodily identification helps him pass through this phase in order to assert his separateness from the internal, omnipotent maternal object. At the same time, his self-preservative aggression toward his archaic maternal imago remains psychically present, and if insufficiently sublimated, obstructs intimate relating and genital-phase progression, oftentimes in the form of misogyny.

As the boy begins to engage in differentiating from the mother (regardless of whether she is "good enough"), she will often continue to experience dramatic shifts in her libidinal life. These libidinal changes typically begin during pregnancy and persist during the period when her primary maternal preoccupation and attunement to her baby are dominant (Winnicott 1956). The actual and unconscious facets of father-with-mother play a prominent role in impacting her relationship with her son's maleness.

The "father in the mother"

The mother's endorsement of her son as a male person tends to operate more unconsciously, and her boy identifies with these unconscious attitudes; this is the paradox of *masculinity-in-femininity* (Ogden 1989). In other words, a boy's elaboration of his masculinity (and triadic object relations) is deficient without a firmly established internal object father carrying the paternal function in the mother's unconscious. The boy's male identification and paternal idealization originate "in a relationship with a woman" (ibid., p. 152).

When a mother is lacking in sufficient mental processes vis-à-vis her male child, the version of himself that the little boy discovers through his mother is tied to more concrete (physical reality) operations that entail defensive strategies to reassure or placate her. In these more pathogenic circumstances, the mother-son attachment is unstable, insecure, and thereby compromised. Without his mother's (and typically his father's) intersubjective recognition of his maleness, such a boy, rather than internalizing a sense of himself as a sexually mentalizing subject with *sexual agency,* develops a gender identity that is defensively based upon his behavioral activity and physical appearance, and thus is formulated in accordance with being a "sex object" (Wilkinson 2001).

In contrast, the mother who identifies with her own securely established internal oedipal father is able to bring the phallic/genital father to the emerging triadic relationship with her son. The unconscious father, or male, in the mother (or in the female analyst) is very much a part of her son's (or patient's) maternal identification. The situation is far more precarious for the son of a mother deficient in this internal object father, who instead is placed in a difficult position from which to psychologically elaborate both his masculinity and his Oedipus complex. This is particularly so when the mother was sexually or physically abused by a father unable to carry the (genital-level) paternal function.

In brief, the boy's sense of masculinity is strongly affected by his mother's feelings about his physicality, sensuality, and temperament, as well as by her endorsement of the father's paternal authority. As I've noted, little boys lacking in this largely unconscious, intersubjective recognition of their maleness establish a highly conflictual internalization of their mothers. For these boys, particularly when the father is emotionally or physically absent—as for example with Brad, the patient discussed in Chapter 3—defensive phallicity or phallic narcissism becomes psychically urgent. In narcissistically valorizing the penis (Braunschweig and Fain 1978), they tend to employ the phallus as a defense and compensate by relying on narcissistic pathology, often featuring perverse sexuality (Herzog 2004).

In my exegesis of the male phallic position in Chapter 3, I stressed such a symbolic use of the phallus as a defense against potential loss of the still-needed maternal object. The unconscious wish to achieve unity with the now-separate mother takes the form of the wish to conquer and possess her while penetrating her body. The boy's phallus becomes his masculine ideal as penis pleasure offers the promise of narcissistic completeness. This phallic power is thus seen as transforming the boy's traumatic separateness from his mother into an increasing influence over her. By adulthood, this "ultimate narcissistic wish for full manhood" (Manninen 1993, p. 36) takes the ideal form of offering one's chosen partner perfect satisfaction, much like Don Juan.

Little boys suffering from more problematic early identifications by and with their mother tend to create a phallic ego ideal and more severe forms of gender splitting to manage the uncontained anxieties arising in such a relational matrix. Such arrested phallicism, marked by a partition in the bodily experience of the sensual from the sexual, operates to stave off intimacy. This is evident with Brad and again with Charles, whom I will discuss later in this chapter.

To restate, then, a securely rooted male identity is largely built upon a boy's *identification with his mother's unconscious attitudes toward his maleness*, a point I have emphasized in previous chapters. A growing boy with this foundation need neither rigidly repress nor disavow feminine identifications in order to differentiate himself (and his still-nascent male gender identity) from his mother (Chodorow 1978). Hence, what a little boy identifies with in his relationship to his mother is the sense of his mother's relating to him as a male person of the opposite sex (Fast 2001; Loewald 1962). In short, a boy's sense of his maleness very much includes the internalization of his mommy's way of relating to him. His internalization of a healthy, sufficiently flexible identity as a male being is greatly influenced by his mother's appreciation of him "as a mentalizing, desiring, and subjective individual" (Wilkinson 2001). It is the mother's (and father's) mental processes pertaining to both his objectivity and his subjectivity that the boy identifies with (Fonagy and Target 1996; Target and Fonagy 2002). Consequently, separation-individuation occurs not because a child disengages from his internalized family objects, but rather, such separation from family objects can ensue only because significant aspects of the boy's relationship to his maternal object have been sufficiently internalized (Behrends and Blatt 1985; Fonagy 2001).

The mother's role in mitigating the boy's separation "trauma" and shame

As noted in Chapter 3, psychoanalysts have cast the boy's experience of separating from his mother's world as his initial preoedipal crisis, or "trauma," conceptualizing it along more traditional, metapsychological lines, emphasizing the loss of an ideal state of primary narcissism and unity with his primary object, or in relational terms that emphasize an interpersonal rupture resulting from the boy's premature loss or repudiation of his sense of connection to his mother. However it is conceptualized, the boy must adapt to the loss just as he is realizing that he is sexually different from his mother. Thus, this loss occurs as he realizes that he can neither *be* the mother nor belong to her female gender—a realization that forms the bedrock trauma for males, "a painful narcissistic mortification … that may have lifelong consequences," as described by Lax (1997, p. 118). Writing along similar lines, Manninen (1992) coined the term *ubiquitous masculine striving* to reflect a man's unconscious drive to discover and reconnect to what has been disavowed and experienced as internally lost in relation to his mother.

From a sociocultural perspective, the boy not only loses a large part of his primary dyadic connection, but he is also pressured to repudiate what he has lost. We saw this in the case of Seth, discussed in Chapter 2. He must deny his need for his mother in order to maintain narcissistic cohesion, whereupon shame unconsciously ensues from his unmet yet intense need for and identification with the maternal object. In general, a boy may feel emotionally abandoned without being aware of it (Pollack 1998), while he is simultaneously culturally prohibited from consciously knowing about or valuing this loss. Normative socialization for males, particularly in the realm of male-to-male relations (Chodorow 2012), relies heavily on the aversive power of shame to shape acceptable male behavior. The need to conform is reinforced through the need to be *independent from his mother* rather than a "momma's boy," "tied to her apron strings," or a "mother fucker," as well as through being *humiliated in relation to other males* as a "pussy, sissy, or faggot." This is most often manifest in defensive efforts against neediness, softness, or being weak. As I've noted, the male psyche can embody an autistic-like, impenetrable citadel in an effort to stave off shame states that are not so easily metabolized (Elise 2001). In short, then, the boy's early separation from his mother is frequently shattering and often traumatic because it results both in an abrupt loss of omnipotence (to be and to have all) and in a prematurely attenuated dyadic connection with his mother.

Often overlooked is the extent to which the boy's unconscious relationship to his masculinity is significantly impacted by both his identification *with* and his identification *by* his mother. Laplanche (1992, 1997, 2007), in contrast, in arguing that the child's unconscious is molded by the unarticulated desires of the adult other through generalized seduction, implies that gender-identity pathologies result from unconsciously transmitted, enigmatic messages imposed upon (assigned to) the developing child, mostly by the mother—much like *ghosts in the nursery* (Fraiberg, Edelson, and Shapiro 1975). The alterity of the mother as other and her inexplicable, polymorphously sexual, and gender-based messages—of which she is mainly unaware—remain somewhat alien and disturbing yet formative of the boy's unconscious. The intromission, implantation, and inscription of these messages—communicated through the language of the body as well as through social and linguistic language—require translation by the male infant/child as a limited hermeneut inexorably inadequate in translating, thereby impacting his sense of masculinity in an ongoing way (Laplanche 2007; Stein 2007).

Accordingly, to reiterate, the mother's unconscious, often unknowable recognition and affirmation of her son's maleness—his identification by his mother and assignment to the male gender, facilitating his self-identification as male in both receptive and penetrating ways—can help him progressively differentiate from her rather than establish his masculinity in violent opposition to her femaleness. As mentioned, Laplanche (2007) refers to this as identification *by* rather than identification *with,* in order to emphasize the primacy of the (m)other in the process. This entails her support for the son's journey toward the world of his father—the world of males. As the boy reaches the period of early triangulation and the phallic stage, the mother's own separation anxieties and oedipal dynamics become crucial, for she must be able to modulate her competitive and envious impulses and contain her more evocatively sensual, erotic desires.

A son who is not supported by his mother when he is turning outward from her while reckoning with his own anatomical incompleteness (further signifying his primordial vulnerability) tends to internalize a particular identification with her—one that in effect opposes his phallic forays toward his father and the external world. This problematic identification, or *phallophobia* (Corbett 2009), operates to impede a boy's healthy aggression, competition, mastery, and authority—as if these qualities would themselves represent an attack on the mother. We see the outcome of a boy's unconscious identification with a competitive, envious, and possibly misandryist mother in our male patients who become attacking and even envious toward their own healthy, assertive, more phallic-like qualities.

Under these circumstances, the place of the father as *third* in the mother's mind, the other of the maternal object (Green 2004; Perelberg 2013), is often empty; instead, the invincible, omnipotent mother seems to have devoured him and may act as if the father has little or no existence for the son (a dynamic that some fathers buy into). Correspondingly, the son's psyche is likely to be characterized by preneurotic, even psychotic structures omnipotently rebelling against the maternal object at the root of a narcissistic mortification (Teising 2008; see also Green 2009). This often results from a crude intrusion on the mother's part (related to orality and anality)—a perverse seduction (Laplanche 1997)—in which a violent variant of mother's implantation, termed *intromission,* dominates, and the necessary separation between her sexuality (as lover) and the act of caring for her child (as nurturer) fails due to the limited paternal function in her mind.

Consequently, rigid, shame-based phallic ideals and severe forms of gender splitting in the form of megalomaniacal fantasies and the illusion of superior male equipment—most evident with Brad, discussed in Chapter 3—are relied upon to manage the shameful, fragmenting anxieties arising in the spheres of sexuality and intimacy. In these circumstances, massive phallic-narcissistic defenses that conceal unrepresentable helplessness, unbinding, and the danger of psychic death (Green 1986) create significant hindrances that resist the integrative work of psychoanalysis.

The attuned mother

The significance of the boy's relationship with his mother cannot be overemphasized. A mother's recognition and affirmation of her son's maleness help him progressively differentiate from her rather than establish his sense of masculinity in violent opposition to her femaleness. By recognition and affirmation of his maleness, I am referring to the mother's capacity to support her son's journey toward the world of his father—the world of males.[1] A mother who is able to contain her own separation anxieties and fears of loss, as well as her envy of the budding son-to-father connection, is better able to support her dyadic relationship with her child. Needless to say, as noted in the preceding section, the mother's oedipal dynamics are crucial, for she must to be able to modulate her own competitive impulses toward the father (as the boy's second other) as they emerge during this early period of triangulation.

Joint parenting by father with mother

An infant is fortunate indeed to have both the mother's ordinary *primary maternal preoccupation* and the father's sufficient *protective agency,* in combination with adequate physical endowment and freedom from unforeseen external trauma. Such an infant is shielded from those primitive annihilation threats to personal self-existence, stemming from experiencing an overwhelming sense of helplessness involving the horrors of falling apart and dissolving, which severely compromise subsequent cognitive, affective, and intrapsychic development. The fetus and then infant provided with "good enough" initial mothering and fathering is thus likely to "go on being," largely unriddled by the more primitive anxieties interfering with each subsequent developmental task (Winnicott 1956, 1980).

It is interesting to keep in mind that it is "the fate of the human psyche to have *always two objects* and never one alone" (Green 1986, p. 146, italics added). Thus, it seems apt to paraphrase Winnicott's (1960) iconic adage and declare that there is no mother without a father, nor any baby without *both* mother and father. Moreover, there can be *no father without the mother's—as well as the child's own (unconscious)—relationship to him.* We are therefore reminded that the core structure of human relatedness is *triangular* (Aisenstein 2015; Eizirik 2015), and the father maintains an ever-present role in the mother's unconscious mind. In recognizing this, psychoanalysts today fully realize a father's influence on his child's reality-based ego functioning and object relations, both in dyadic (preoedipal) and triadic (oedipal) paternal countenance (Diamond 2007, 2015).

Establishing the paternal function in traditional triadic familial systems

The father's potential involvement, as well as his actual and symbolic influence, always operates within a family context and a cultural and socioeconomic milieu. The mother (or her substitute) typically acts as gatekeeper to fatherhood and, consequently, she plays a crucial role in either supporting or obstructing the father's active engagement with the child, as well as the nature of the child's attachment to him. As the first clinical example at the end of this chapter—describing the case of Charles—suggests, specific conflicts and deficits occur in the absence of sufficient fathering by dint of either the mother's or the child's internal banishment of the father. This loss of the actual and symbolic father is manifest in the painful affective state of longing for the father, the *fathersehnsucht* that has been termed *father hunger* (Herzog 1982a, 2001).

The mother's conscious and unconscious attitudes toward the father—the father's representation in the mother's mind and expressed in her discourse—partly reflect qualities in the unconscious relationship to her own father. This factor is crucial to the child's ability to internalize the father's healthy presence, along with the paternal function itself. Mothers play a significant role in furthering the passage from the narcissistic to the symbolic father, and in this respect, they also help separate the child from the father to become "Daddy's little man" or "Daddy's little girl" (Diamond 2015; Perelberg 2013). However, we need not assume that the mother simply internalizes the actual father's paternal function; rather, as I've noted, the task of separating herself from the child may be carried out by the mother as a result of her own desire (Diamond 2015; Glocer Fiorini 2013). In fact, this symbolic function is often owned by the mother as a subject herself.

Ideally in traditional family systems, children need to experience their parents as a couple in an interactive, nontraumatic partnership, or parenting alliance (Diamond 1986). The beneficial effect of the highly involved father is thus primarily the result of there being two caregivers, which produces a better-functioning familial system. This enables the child to construct a representational "trialogue" of self-with-mother, self-with-father, and self-with-mother-and-father-together (Herzog 2009)—representations that are continually reworked and reconstructed throughout life's vicissitudes and developmental phases.

The mother who is able to keep the father alive in her own mind, regardless of whether or not he is actually present and involved, absent, or dead—in contrast to the mother who mentally banishes or expels (i.e., "murders") the father—provides the child with a healthy triangular representation that facilitates internalization of the paternal function. To reiterate, this is particularly helpful in the establishment of the child's sense of gender and sexual identity.

A vital feature of the traditional, Westernized parental-couple-and-child triad pertains to the child's internalization of a healthy father/mother representation—namely, an internal fatherly imago that partially depends on the nature of the father-mother relationship as it interfaces with the child's predispositions acquired through intergenerational transmission (Faimberg 2004). Children carry this representation of father-with-mother in ways that powerfully impact later romantic intimacies throughout life.

The crucial role of mother-with-father together parenting

Trustworthy yet restraining fathers enable triadic object relations to mature as the son takes on the role of one parent in relation to the other in a conflicted way. In the preeminent phallic-oedipal representation of triadic object relations, the son shifts from being mother's baby to being her lover and from being father's baby to being his competitor and companion.

Many men with absent or less involved fathers—such as Jake, the second clinical case described later in this chapter—who have had difficulties in asserting themselves within the domestic domain will need to face their own tendencies to withdraw from familial conflict in order to father their sons (and daughters) well. Analytic treatment is often useful for men inclined to automatically turn away from potential conflict; instead, they can learn to reengage when more avoidant impulses take hold. This necessitates admitting to oneself the ways in which a sense of being a "reluctant" man or father—particularly in holding and fulfilling the symbolic, paternal function (what is often termed "manning up")—is carried inside, often dating back to one's own father's parenting style. Consequently, instead of withdrawing from potentially volatile conflict, the father can be helped to assert a paternal perspective on his children's needs as well as his own. He may also successfully reestablish the parenting alliance with his wife or partner as he becomes more assertive in child rearing. During phases of a son's efforts to individuate, this often requires supporting the wife while still recognizing and affirming the son's attempt to forge his own identity.

In other words, fathers frequently need to do what is necessary to champion their sons' development. This may entail helping the mother become better able to recognize, support, and affirm her son's maleness—aiding her in not being threatened by the son's aggression and separation needs and in not becoming hateful of men in general. Such paternal functioning in triadic reality helps raise sons with fewer internal conflicts in these domains.

For example, an involved father can teach his partner about parenting boys by stepping in to normalize their son's burgeoning masculinity. In this respect, the father serves as a translator, interpreting the son's behavior so that the mother can understand it and place it within a helpful context. A father who can negotiate this deeper understanding of his son with his spouse strengthens their parenting alliance. Under these favorable circumstances, regardless of the son's age, a son is more likely to experience himself as a good son who is loved by a good mother and a good father together. I have observed that sons who carry this triangular sense of worthiness are more able to enter into loving and committed relationships with suitable partners.

In the final analysis, both parents need to support their son's ties to the other parent. If they don't, the son's masculine sense of worth will likely be damaged. In considering such paternal functioning to support a son's healthy tie to his mother, Ducat (2004) writes: "Boys who grow up in these circumstances are less destructively envious of mothers and other women, more able to embrace identification with both mothers and fathers, less fearful and disparaging of women and the 'feminine' in themselves, and less inclined to engage in hypermasculine acting out in adulthood" (p. 58).

The symbolic father's function and triangularity in analytic interactions

When space for symbolic functioning is opened, the Law of the Father within analytic space is established (Lacan 1966, 2005), and the paternal third supplements and complements the unconscious early mother-child pair by containing the oedipal triangle and facilitating symbolic experience (Britton 1989). Thus, the establishment of appropriate intimacy between patient and analyst is helped by the patient's early experiences of healthy relationships with both mother and father. A deeper, more meaningful connection between patient and analyst requires that they be "touched" by one another's otherness in an analytic way. This more intimate contact can proceed only when the paternal order supplements the maternal order rooted in the early mother-child dyad (Bollas 2000, 2011)—which means that the patient's ability to locate the self within a triadic matrix is key to the development of a robust analytic relationship.

As I will discuss in Chapter 8, the analyst, too, must draw on his or her psychic maturity and healthy sense of triangulation in developing the capacity to hold both maternal and paternal states of mind that together fertilize the patient's developing capacity for intimate relationships. In other words, the analyst's binocular, or *bi-ocular*, mode of attentiveness—which maintains an interplay between the maternal and the paternal by "holding the immediate and something other" (Birksted-Breen 2016, p. 36)—establishes the necessary triangulation for "engendering new thoughts" (p. 31). In this respect, the analytic process is facilitated by both the analyst's bigenderality and his/her gender fluidity.

In addition to well-established capacities for triangulation (Zweibel 2004), the analyst must be capable of more developed symbolic thinking, and he or she must have the self-containment necessary to bear his/her own experiences without understanding them (Caper 2017). In short, the analyst must skillfully employ his/her own analytic mind to transform weakly symbolized material into an interpretable or simply bearable form (Diamond 2014). Thus, the analyst's integrative, representational, meaning-making, and self-containing operations convey a paternal quality, in contrast to the analyst's more receptive, less integrated, and relaxed symbolic capabilities that represent maternal containment.

The following two case examples illustrate the impact of insufficient triangularity in the mother-with-father-with-son triad. In the first example, that of Charles, the mother's degradation of the fathering function (along with the father's abdication of such functioning) results in a collusive relationship between mother and son that impedes the son's sexuality and capacity for intimacy. The second case, that of Jake, indicates the profound impact on a son's maturation and fathering capacity stemming from the mother's failure to attune to her son's maleness, in conjunction with a negligent father's failure to help his son transition away from the maternal orbit.

The case of Charles: colluding with mother against father[2]

Charles, a 44-year-old married man, was severely impaired in his ability to integrate his tender and sensuous impulses—as well as his aggression—toward his loved objects. He had grown up engaged with his mother in a collusive degradation of his father that essentially precluded the paternal function (carried by neither mother nor father). Consequently, Charles was unable to progress from his exclusive dyadic relationship with mother to find a place within triadic reality.

As an only child, he felt greatly adored by his mother, who had consistently demeaned his father, a depressed man who had been hospitalized subsequent to a breakdown when Charles was about four years old. Soon thereafter, the father left the marriage, making contact again with Charles only during his teenage years. After the divorce, his mother did not remarry or even date.

Given his mother's adoration, her contempt for his disturbed father (which Charles collusively embraced), and her attack on the paternal function itself, the role of a needed paternal figure in both symbolic and actual functioning was largely missing in what might be considered father murder. Nonetheless, Charles sought to create an internal father who would protect him from his mother (thereby reducing his merger anxieties). However, because he remained fixated on an unconscious fantasy of a *murdered father*, his efforts contributed to his symptom, and he unconsciously made his absent, weak father into a dangerously castrating man in an attempt to prop up the paternal function and omnipotently create the Law. His development of a ruthlessly punitive superego made his life a miserable one in which he had little hope of emotional fulfillment or happiness given his impairments in the realms of sexuality and aggression.

Lacking a father able to fulfill the paternal function of helping his son separate from his mother, Charles became impaired in his ability to regulate his own erotic desires and aggression. Thus, while remaining poorly differentiated from his engulfing and omnipresent mother, Charles, in his hysterical countenance, experienced himself as "stuck and unable to become a grown man." Partly as a result of lacking the symbolic (and genital) father, Charles could not allow himself to experience desire or pleasure when having sex with his wife, whom he described as "dominating yet very loving" (i.e., his purified and engulfing mother), given the unconsciously imagined danger. Instead, only with prostitutes or when compulsively masturbating to sadomasochistic images could he dare to engage the carnal, aggressive features of his sexuality; only these activities allowed him to reach orgasm.

When directed toward his much-loved wife, Charles's masculine sexuality produced an incest-based, terrifying emotional flooding that severely restricted his intimate coupling. Freud (1910) described this as the *Madonna/whore* complex in which a splitting of the (maternal) object occurs wherein the mother's "unimpeachable moral purity" (p. 169) is contrasted with a prostitute's. Hence, in lacking the symbolic father, Charles could not allow himself to experience desire or pleasure when having sex with his wife (i.e., his purified and engulfing mother), given the unconsciously imagined danger.

Through experiences in the transference-countertransference, I came to understand that, in addition to the largely missing *actual* father, Charles's access to the *symbolic* father, whom he needed to separate him from the unconscious dangers of a mother merger, was severely restricted. He remained blocked in his development while with his mother, often through an identification with her narcissistic omnipotence as the "phallic" mother. Simultaneously, however, as a result of his projected reactive and primitive aggression, he greatly feared her vengeful power.

Later in the treatment, this became clearer in the transference, wherein Charles attempted to remain in what he would call "a safe bubble," in which I, as his analyst, needed to be "completely attuned" to him (while Charles simultaneously sought to conform to what he thought I wanted from him). During these periods, he would often speak about feeling safely enveloped in a "womblike cloud," reminiscing about how, throughout his childhood, he would often lie on his mother's lap as she stroked his hair and soothed him until he peacefully drifted off to sleep. Meanwhile, within our dyad, however, any unwelcome silences, breathing, coughing, or sneezing sounds, and/or perceived moments of distraction on my part, were felt to impinge upon this bubble and disrupt his perception of safety. Since any such occurrences seemed to reveal my lack of interest, empathy, or care, he would subtly berate me as "breaking into" his world and leaving him utterly alone in an unbearable state.

In response, I would feel useless in my (fusional) effort to relieve his suffering while unable to understand what was happening. My mind would frequently shut down, and it increasingly became very challenging to accept Charles's projections and nonetheless experience myself as an inner object who could capably think sufficiently to pull both of us out of our fusional projective identification in order to shed light on a situation that encompassed gaps between our minds.

For long periods of time during these mutual enactments, Charles would often become withdrawn and (spitefully) silent. However, once I could recover my analytic mind—largely by rediscovering the oedipal, triadic dimension in my experience with him, particularly when I could consider the meaning of my disturbing experience while bearing the disruptive gaps between us without fully understanding them—I became better able to find the *third* within me in order to detach from what was occurring between us. Consequently, I could interpret the absence inside him that caused him to feel so disrupted whenever he experienced my being engaged in something that did not include him. At such moments, Charles could begin to take in this understanding and, perhaps indicative of launching a mourning process, he soon replied with considerable emotion in describing his feeling of "being dropped and therefore very unsafe."

The significance of a persistent attack on the paternal function that would have upheld the task of separating the child from the maternal orbit (and that could be carried either within the mother and/or assumed by the father's presence, depending on the individual situation) is illustrated by a session with Charles in which the following exchange took place. Sensing my thoughtful reflection about his description of his wife's angry reproaches concerning his lack of sexual interest in her, Charles blurted out, spontaneously and rather uncharacteristically, "I hate your damn thinking—stop it, I'm sick of it; just tell me how to satisfy her!"

Understanding that my "thinking" disrupted his dyadic merger with me, I said that my thinking, and even my unwelcome breathing or coughing at times, broke into the bubble that he felt we existed in together—a bubble like the one he had created with his mother.

Charles quickly pointed out that he could not feel "safe" with me if I was not "empathic" with him. Now that I could more easily see how triangular space in the analytic situation threatened Charles by causing him to experience himself as located too separately outside my internal world, I replied: "It seems quite dangerous to you if I enter from outside 'the bubble'—making you feel left completely alone and uncared for, with no one, especially me, to turn to." I then added, "If I seem to be 'thinking,' you realize at some level that I could be in dialogue with some part of me that is not accessible to you—as if the 'mother-me' is engaged with someone else, and that leaves you out."

As Charles's anger subsided, he became tearful, and we soon began to discuss his lack of a father who could be present and differentiated from his mother and her disparaging stories about him. I added, "You needed that anger to manage the anxiety of being without a father when you emerged from the 'bubbly world' with mother." "Yeah, I know this is true," he said, then added in a worried voice, "But I'm feeling really uncomfortable talking about this."

Charles then quite anxiously began to recount the trauma of his father's actual abandonment, along with his painful hunger for a father. As a result of his becoming able to verbalize these feelings, his traumatizing abandonment increasingly became interpretable, as did his defensive use of the maternal merger in a collusive effort to abolish the paternal function.

Months later, when the missing paternal third had become a more active, less resisted-against element in the analytic dyad, Charles seemed quite sad and yet less anxious. Entering further into the depressive position (taken up by Klein [1935] as the primitive oedipal situation), he began to speak in a mourning tone of the lost illusion of his bubble—the all-embracing, eternally protective mother who would shield him from the slings and arrows of life, including his father's traumatizing abandonment. Triangular space in the analytic situation was opening up through the activation of the paternal function within the analytic relationship, and Charles wondered aloud if he needed pornography to "avoid being more open" with his wife.

Brief case discussion

This case illustrates the impact of the abolishment of a paternal function capable of breaking the little boy's collusive maternal tie and thereby establishing a healthier form of triangularity. As with many of the patients described by Perelberg (2015), for Charles, there was an inability to shift from *murdered father* to *dead father*. Due to the absence of the dead father, only the murdered, narcissistic father could dwell in Charles's psyche; consequently, the fundamental psychic progression from concrete to symbolic functioning and from dyadic to triadic structure was prevented.

In contrast to Charles's triadic matrix, however, a different dynamic is established when the father who serves as the intervening third, separator of mother-child, and representation of the paternal function (i.e., Lacan's

Law of the Father) helps dislodge the child's center of gravity from within the mother to within the child's self. Hence, by coming between mother and child, the father helps establish the child's subjectivity, capacity to symbolize, and thinking itself—all part of the child's separate, individuating self. Because the father-in-the-mother as well as an actual father-with-mother was lacking, Charles remained severely limited in his capacity to achieve a genital position that enabled him to experience mature intimacy with an other. Through the analytic process and the analyst's functioning as *third*, however, a much-needed symbolic father function was established, and eventually, Charles was able to give up pornography and return to his wife's bed.

The case of Jake: triangulation deficiency due to paternal neglect and maternal failure[3]

Jake, a 40-year-old married man, sought treatment because of his extreme overly protective anxieties concerning his then-three-year-old son's welfare. He could barely leave the house for work each day because he trusted no one other than his working wife to care for the boy.

Jake's anxieties stemmed from his early history as an only child. His father had seemingly dedicated his life to his very successful business that required working sixteen-hour days, traveling worldwide, and spending weekends engaged in business-related social activities. Jake rarely saw his father, and his alcoholic mother was depressed and emotionally unavailable except at bedtime. Nannies and babysitters were primarily in charge of Jake's welfare, though tragically, a male babysitter repeatedly abused him sexually between the ages of four and eight. Neither Jake's absent father nor his depressed mother was able to protect him, nor to help him process or metabolize the abuse. Years later, when his father was told of the molestation, he refused to believe that such a thing could occur in their own home. Adhering to a rigid, traditional notion of phallic masculinity that entailed renouncing even paternal desire itself, he professed that Jake was "always too sensitive and not strong enough to handle things in the real world."

Despite feeling inadequate and frightened, the artistically talented Jake excelled academically, was sent away from home in his early teens to attend boarding school, and generally grew up as quickly as possible. Today, although married and seemingly successful in his profession, Jake lives in quiet terror and agonizing solitude. His pain is poignantly captured by William Blake's words from "Little Boy Lost" (1789): "Father, father, where are you going?/O do not walk so fast./Speak father, speak to your little boy/Or else I shall be lost" (p. 11).

Although he described his mother as "miserable and unavailable" when he was a small child, Jake nonetheless believed he was "the most important person in the world to her." She told him that his father "didn't want children," and that she didn't care that his father traveled so much "as long as she had me—especially at bedtime when Dad was away." He recalled sleeping in her bed, often watching her parade in front of him in only her bra and panties, and remembered hearing that his father had other "girlfriends," while proudly feeling that as a precious child, he was his mother's "boyfriend."

Jake felt that his father always seemed big and slightly dangerous; he noted that on the rare occasions when he was home, his dad would have "huge temper tantrums when anything wasn't the way he wanted it." Though frightened, Jake experienced safety in being allied with his mother against his explosive father. The absence of an actual, mature father capable of fulfilling the paternal function, coupled with his mother's inability to recognize his actual maleness and parent him appropriately, interacted with Jake's unconsciously murderous oedipal impulses.

What became most pronounced in the transference was that Jake suffered from the lack of a paternal third who could say "no" both to Jake and to his mother's desire to avoid losing her magical union with her tiny Narcissus, and thereby introduce him to the realm of sacrifice, renunciation, and the mourning of omnipotent wishes. Although his biological father was alive (if emotionally distant), Jake's internal world lacked the needed symbolic father function to facilitate his individuation; hence, he was poorly equipped to develop the capacity to bear the inevitable tensions of incompleteness—a capacity that was required for him to leave his mother's bed.

This lack became particularly evident in the analytic field, and for a considerable period, it seemed as if I didn't exist for Jake in my own right, as if I were a fully merged (maternal) part of him concurring with whatever he said or did. I had little to say or do (but show up), and he seemed to look right through me while speaking aloud only to himself.

I could certainly make sense of why Jake had major difficulties in fathering his own child, let alone in regulating himself as an adult male in the world. Men, in particular, when lacking both their father's involved presence and the paternal function, tend to suffer in the realm of their own aggression, ambition, and feel for authority and power (Diamond 2007). In fact, Jake revealed around this time that his son, now five, was still not toilet trained. Jake had no idea how to set realistic limits for the boy because he could not do so for himself. In addition, it came to light that his apparently successful business was actually a sham. His borrowing on credit was coming apart, lies were being exposed (including a secret affair and prescription drug misuse), and his marriage was about to break up as he filed for bankruptcy. His wish to cover up the truth—his turning a blind eye to reality (Steiner 1985)—often trumped his desire to know himself.

I increasingly felt frustrated and frequently felt the urge to confront him aggressively about his slippery, duplicitous presentations. Still, Jake's psychic bankruptcy was most troubling as he seemed unable to represent himself either with his father or with his mother and father together, thus severely impairing his ability to live within his current family triad. Consequently, left with only a lost, missing, and murdered father, Jake remained psychically merged with his mother, unable to relinquish his fusional wishes in order to navigate in the world.

Jake's narrative eventually began to focus on behavioral problems that he wanted to solve through my "coaching" him as to what to do pertaining to his son's toileting difficulties, his wife's irritating "nagging" about his business failing, and his constant mismanagement of his finances. I struggled with my own annoyance and began to have fantasies of brutally confronting him with his ineptitude. I couldn't stand listening to him passively describe what seemed to "just happen" as he innocently—and ineptly—tried to manage his son, his wife, and his money.

In time, however, it became clearer that what needed to be brought to light lay within my countertransference—namely, I had to understand that Jake was stuck as a tragically forlorn little boy who desperately longed for a father to simply tell him what to do. Before breaking through the logjam as my own feelings of hopelessness and despair mounted, treatment had come to an impasse wherein for several months I had to suffer through Jake's persistent attacks on the treatment—including threatening to end it while contacting a former therapist who "always made me feel good."

The beginnings of a breakthrough occurred one evening when I had a dream involving a life-and-death struggle to pull myself out of a small, sinking ship without any rope or life raft. I felt like I was drowning and woke up very disturbed, my thoughts turning to Jake. In associating to my dream, I recognized that my own paternal functioning was under collusive attack (by both of us). Though I had inevitably been drawn into the reciprocal orbit of projective identification, I started to realize that for both our sakes, I needed to pull myself out from the morass of an unconscious merger on a "sinking ship."

The attacks, including "splitting of the transference," while overdetermined in reflecting both a form of oedipal competition and perhaps negative therapeutic reaction, also represented Jake's longing to find (within the transference) an involved yet challenging paternal presence (i.e., the paternal law), a surviving father function that could break into the fusional maternal transference to establish triadic reality, with its generational succession and emergent capacity to sacrifice an idealized, omnipotent sense of wholeness.

Consequently, I soon began interpreting Jake's attacks as an unconscious plea for some sort of fatherly law that would help him disengage from his merger within the maternal orbit. I added that he feared I wouldn't survive, which would again leave him without a strong and capable internal figure—without a "fatherly analyst" who could help him face himself. Though he often became quite agitated during these sessions, accusing me of trying to control him, he nonetheless cried rather often as he began recalling memories of his childhood longings for his father to return, catch him sleeping with his mother, and promptly pull him out of her bed. Not surprisingly, rather than terminating the treatment, he increased our sessions to thrice weekly at this time, while confessing that he actually knew how to solve more of his problems than he let on. For the first time in our three years of working together, our sessions came alive and began moving forward, though the road ahead would remain a bumpy one.

Brief case discussion

It is implicit that, in addition to the irrefutable benefits of engaged fathering that can successfully ride the inevitable tides of rivalry, neglect, and desire, the father functioning as a third within the analytic dyad—as the work with Jake illustrates—helps create a wider analytic frame, protecting against therapeutic symbiosis. The analyst's functioning in this way also guards against the basic assumptions of pairing that provides a false "Messiah, be it a person, idea, or Utopia" (Bion 1961, p. 152). Similar to Freud's suggestion of psychoanalysis as a cure through transference love (1907), paternal love, in its capacity to maintain the separating function (i.e., the Law of the Father) within the analytic situation through recognition of the other's uniqueness, may help "cure" both analyst and patient (Diamond 2017a).

Both the attuned mother who is able to support her son's phallic forays and the involved father who is able to hold the symbolic function—primarily by regulating his incestuous and rivalrous, aggressive, as well as narcissistic impulses—help make what is perhaps the most important contribution to their child's future. The result of such successful mother-with-father triadic involvement greatly increases the likelihood that their sons (and daughters) will construct and later retain an internal sense of being recognized as both *separate from others* and *with others* as they capably face life's challenges, tolerating its absences and limitations, and renouncing certain desires in order to remain vibrantly alive.

Unfortunately, neither Charles nor Jake could develop the healthy sense of maleness that emerges from a sufficiently functioning triadic familial system. However, both men were able to make use of the analytic process to develop their triadic functioning by means of breaking through the collusive internalized dyad, which allowed them to move forward in maturing manhood.

Notes

1 A more pathological maternal identification is established for the son through the mother's unconscious limitation in recognizing and sanctioning her boy's maleness, as well as her husband's fatherliness—a limitation evident in Greenson's (1968) case of Lance (discussed in Chapter 1) and in my own work with Seth (Chapter 2) and Charles (later in this chapter).
2 I have discussed Charles in a previous article (Diamond 2017b).
3 I have discussed Jake in a previous article (Diamond 2018).

6 Social, cultural, and biological influences on the concepts of masculinity and gender: constructing the male ego ideal

In this chapter, cultural ideals of manhood are explored in terms of their influence on the gender identity development of both boys and girls. Dichotomies in gender identity are recognized, as well as the need to re-concile binary traits and tendencies in establishing a healthy gender identity that goes beyond prevailing heteronormative models. Relevant findings from neuroscience and biology help us compare and contrast the early childhood development of males with that of females. The concept of the *ego ideal* is employed as a tool with which to examine the specific impact of sociocultural and biological influences on the psychodynamics of male patients. I maintain that these influences converge to confirm that masculinity remains tenuous for all males, whether straight, gay, or bisexual, while always involving loss and lifelong tensions related to gendered ego ideals. A brief clinical vignette illustrates the distinct oedipal challenges that a man must confront to attain a maturing *genital ego ideal* through the analytic relationship.

An ideological evolution

As I have indicated, both psychoanalysis and prevailing cultural ideas about masculinity have changed and developed substantially—somewhat in parallel fashion—over the past century. Each has been constructed from and restricted by the masculine/feminine binary—as well as by heteronormative norms—that led to a theory and practice centered on the idea that masculinity depends upon the overvaluation of phallicity and the successful repudiation of the feminine. Cultural ideals of manhood, partially rooted in biological factors, greatly influence the gender identity development of both boys and girls. Although gendered identity is always constituted out of the *sexed body, sexuality and desire*, and *social/cultural ideals, impositions, and inscriptions*, what is most significant for us as psychoanalysts is the *unconscious psychic investment in*, and *fantasies pertaining to*, each of these domains.

Before discussing the inherent tensions that arise for males within the gender binary, I will turn briefly to the present-day, Westernized cultural domain to consider less traditional men and the escalating attempt to contravene the binary.

Less traditional males: a note on transgressing the binary

As I noted in Chapter 2, theorization of gender and psychosexuality is rooted in the binary of *"phallic logic ... of presence/absence, of zero and one"* (Laplanche 2007, p. 217, italics added).[1] Yet, of course, there are children and adults who transgress the gender binary, and we are increasingly called upon to consider that there may be something beyond the so-called "hetero-normative vision of psychic bisexuality" (Gulati and Pauley 2019, p. 109). When one operates from the binary vision of only two sexes or genders, any alternative proposition tends to be regarded as a reluctance to accept finitude and relinquish omnipotence. Some analysts consider this tendency the privi-leging of *cisgender heteronormativity* (Gherovici 2019). In contrast, there are a few non-Western cultures in which a "third sex" outside the two genders or sexes is part of the cultural fabric (Gulati and Pauley 2019).

Even in Westernized societies, there are an increasing number of ways of constructing gender, and psychoanalysts have posited a far more complex re-lationship between gender, sexuality, the body, and the social than was once envisioned (Cereijido 2019). Parallel to radical alterations in sociocultural gender roles and complexities, concepts pertaining to gender identity as well as to gender itself are increasingly being questioned, both in public debate and in psychoanalytic discourse. Steven Seidman and Alan Frank (2019), two socio-logically oriented psychoanalysts, aptly consider how gender is being re-imagined beyond *cisgendered heteronormativity*, which is signified by such binary-avoidant notions as "metrosexual, queer, genderqueer, ... ungendered, agender, ... polygendered, trans*, third gender, transgendered, pangendered, and gender non-conforming" (p. 20). In short, contemporary psychoanalysis recognizes that our genders are, in Adrienne Harris's (2005) words, "softly assembled," and characterized by plasticity, fluidity, and tensions related to social transformations in a rapidly changing gender environment.[2]

The inherent tension of the gender binary

Arguably, as anthropologist-psychoanalyst Rozine Perelberg (2018) sug-gests, the binary characterized by phallic logic is universal, since the phallus/no phallus is "an inherent characteristic of all human beings" (p. 2). This *cultural* (rather than *biological*) given produces useful, albeit limiting dichotomies, including masculine/feminine, phallic/castrated, active/pas-sive, heterosexual/homosexual, and even male/female itself. However, de-spite being more frequently experienced as a site of personal choice and more "plastic than hardwired" (Seidman and Frank 2019, p. 20), the no-tion of gender identity has proved to be enduring even while grasped less tightly. I agree with Dominique Scarfone's (2019) idea that, because we tend to live *in the binary,* deviations from the male/female dichotomy re-quire considerable efforts that render it difficult to "carry [them] over to everyday parlance" (p. 572). Consequently, almost every human being must inevitably struggle with "the apparent binariness of sex-gender (including gender role and sexuality)" (Barratt 2019, p. 14).[3]

To return to the masculine gender, the leading factor in the sociocultural domain, as I highlighted in previous chapters, is the idea that masculinity depends upon the overvaluation of phallicity, which itself is built on successfully repudiating what is equated with or coded as the feminine. However, this primarily culturally influenced renunciation leads to psychic (and, too often, material) violence wherein the feminine is targeted both internally and externally. Consequently, emerging psychic structure pertaining to gender identity tends to be compromised for males who create unconscious gender-based ego ideals.

I will elaborate in this chapter on ideas pertaining to cultural as well as biological, embodied influences on the largely unconscious and invariably conflicted nature of the male's gendered identity.

Cultural ideals of manhood: the impact of the heteronormative model

Along with several other analytic writers (Axelrod 1995; Chodorow 2012; Elise 2001; Seidman and Frank 2019), I believe that it is necessary to address the cultural element in understanding the ubiquity of the masculine striving (and the ego ideals that underlie this). Societal standards of manhood function on both cultural and individual levels, and hence important data stems from both anthropology and sociology. For instance, Gilmore (1990) examined traditional injunctions to achieve "real manhood" across cultures and concluded there to be a "deep structure" of masculinity that is encouraged by a range of rituals and manhood ideals. From his retrospective cross-cultural findings, it has emerged that the vast majority of cultures perpetuate a male role with three main functions: to *impregnate*, to *protect*, and to *provide*.

Among contemporary Westernized men, the protective, providing father imago reflects duties emblematic of such constantly sought manhood. Although we cannot know the biological or archetypal basis of this paternal depiction with certitude, it seems evident that this idealization of the father as a *delegate of the outside world* operates powerfully as a cultural representation, even when the real parents do not reinforce it (Benjamin 1988). Moreover, although gender role expectations are in transition, for many men and even some career-oriented women, there remains a conventional expectation that the man serves as the primary provider or breadwinner. At least until more recently, the *protective, providing paternal representation* tends to predominate even when traditional gender divisions in parenting, in which the mother is the primary nurturing figure, are modified (Pruett 1987).[4]

Whereas addressing the cultural dimension is useful, from our psychoanalytic perspective, it is crucial to recognize that the concept of *gender identity* is far more complex than assumed when so often approached as though it is based on social processes and conscious choices. Thinking analytically, *identity* is always connected with *unconscious fantasy and sexuality* (Lemma 2018), whereas the issue of *gender* is aptly regarded as an *essential contradiction* (Harris 1991). Rather than simply deconstructing gender dichotomies, I believe that sophisticated psychoanalytic theory must be able to sustain the necessary dialectical tension between traditional *essentialist* (either/or) thinking and a postmodern, *constructivist* (both/and) perspective.

To reiterate, then, there is a tension between biological givens, such as hormonally influenced brain and bodily masculinization, and the psychosocially created. Gender *theory* requires explaining "how the tension between fixed and fluid aspects … can be held on to rather than foreclosed" (Sweetnam 1996, p. 449). At the same time, *analytic praxis* necessitates entertaining a range of internal psychic positions consisting of multiple, contradictory, and shifting gender-related identifications and internalizations with which to reflect on a particular patient's relationship with his or her more consciously accessible sense of gender.[5]

Still, as cultural beings, we cannot so easily contain this tension. Anthropologists write about a ubiquitous sociocultural process that effectively splits gender traits so that aspects of human personality are distributed unequally between the sexes. In every culture, the individual internalizes a *culturally shaped gender polarity* that directs him or her to develop qualities attributed to his or her own sex and, in some measure, to suppress qualities of the other sex (Labouvie-Vief 1994; Young-Eisendrath 1997).

This culturally based polarity occurs even though hormonal influences on the fetal brain and genitalia demonstrate differences between the two genders. Regardless of how we define the concepts of *masculine* and *feminine* from a constitutional perspective, what is most serviceable in psychoanalysis stems from clinical observation, as Freud argued in differentiating men from women. In his words, "pure masculinity or femininity is *not* to be found in either a psychological or a biological sense. Every individual, on the contrary, displays a mixture of the character-traits belonging to his own and to the opposite sex; and he shows a combination of *activity and passivity* whether or not these last character-traits tally with his biological ones" (1905, p. 220n, italics added).

Because culture always plays a pivotal role in shaping the psychodynamics of gender identity, gender binaries remain highly significant in clinical psychoanalytic treatment. In treating a male patient, the primary focus for most analysts tends to be on the parents in relation to their son and to one another; nonetheless, sibling and peer relations, the *boy culture* with its enforced male code privileging a particular binary that every boy encounters growing up, must be kept in mind as we try to understand each unique male patient.

In Western societies, despite efforts to reduce this gender splitting, the underlying cultural images for masculine behavior generally continue to involve being rational, protective, aggressive, and dominating, while those for femininity incorporate being emotional, nurturing, receptive, and submissive (Benjamin 1988; Fogel 1998). It becomes each individual's burden to keep the other gender's characteristics less developed within—and particularly so, as I will indicate, for males who remain especially vulnerable to feeling humiliated in relation to other males (Chodorow 2012; Kaftal 1991).

In considering how such sociocultural factors impact male gender identity and the male's unconsciously constructed ego ideals, I will begin by contrasting boys with girls.

How do boys compare with girls?

It is interesting to contrast boys with girls at the time of their initial gender differentiation in confronting the fact of sexual difference during the second or third year. Young boys tend to be less mature cognitively and emotionally than little girls, and their developmental timetable is slower. There is typically another developmental asymmetry, in that little boys are *pressured to renounce gender-inconsistent traits* far more than young girls are; this seems to be more so for proto-gay boys who are coerced to repudiate or severely inhibit their homoerotic desires when living in a traditional, compulsory heteronormative world (Frommer 2000; Gonzalez 2013). In fact, by age six, boys—whether proto-straight or proto-gay—experience considerably less gender constancy (i.e., the feeling of remaining the same gender regardless of changes in appearance, affect, or behavior) than do girls (Fast 1984; Hansell 1998).

Consistent with my positing heightened primordial vulnerability among males, as discussed in Chapter 3, it seems that infant boys have a more limited capacity for self-regulation, are more impacted by mother-infant attachment failures in containment and regulatory functioning, and require earlier maternal (and/or paternal) co-regulation than do girls. As also noted and as I will elaborate later in this chapter, males seem to be more vulnerable to maternal psychopathology and suffer their incompleteness within the maternal dyad more severely than do girls. Moreover, developmental research demonstrates that taboos against cross-gender behavior tend to be enforced much more brutally by parents, peers, and society generally when the behavior is exhibited by boys (Maccoby 1998). As I've implied, there are also greater prohibitions against early homoerotic attachments and homosexuality for boys; as they mature, boys show considerable inhibition against reexperiencing their early maternal erotic attachment (we saw this with Seth, the patient discussed in Chapter 2).

Due to heightened shame associated with homoeroticism and father hunger, boys also have difficulty with erotic desires directed toward their fathers, as well as toward other males. Proto-gay boys experience themselves as "outsiders" upon beginning their oedipal journeys, often in response to their fathers' anxious detachment (Isay 1989). Unlike girls, boys are inescapably called upon to safely negotiate a passage through the dangers of this *traumatic discovery of otherness* (Ogden 1989). As elaborated in Chapter 3, boys do not grow up experiencing themselves as masculine by dint of being male; *masculinity has to be won*—and, typically, *proven repeatedly.*

Such shame dynamics carry the sense of being exposed as weak should any needs become evident; these dynamics develop directly from the boy's abrupt sense of defectiveness during his preoedipal experience of separation, entailing feelings of helplessness, weakness, and vulnerability. To restate, then, the boy's repudiation of femininity—Freud's (1937) underlying bedrock—reflects his refusal of the primitive dependence on (and his even less accessible longing to return to) the mother. As discussed in Chapter 3, it is the male's *primordial vulnerability* and necessary reliance on maternal care that produces his terrors of being engulfed by the archaic feminine (Chasseguet-Smirgel 1964; Cournut 1998; Green 1986). Under these conditions in the more patriarchal, phallocentric cultures that most psychoanalysts work in, the phallic boy and often the adult male (as for instance Brad, the patient discussed in Chapter 3), in trying to find a solution to his experience of lack, resorts to a denial of lack—namely, a *lack of lacking*—rather than accepting it (Lacan 1962).

Nonetheless, however, the psyche is located in the body—we are *embodied* by nature—and it becomes every individual's challenge to achieve what has been described as "the psyche indwelling in the soma" (Winnicott 1960, p. 589). Because there is always some evidence for biological influences, we need to consider the part that biology might play in its intersection with the aforementioned cultural imperatives to produce our unconscious and conflicted gendered identity.

Biological factors: findings from neuroscience

There is sizeable research indicating biological differences between males and females that seems significant for psychoanalysis, such as described in the writings of Jaak Panksepp (1998), Simon Baron-Cohen (2003, 2007), and Edward Tronick (2007). On the whole, sex differences in the brain are reflected in somewhat differing maturational timetables in that girls are slightly more advanced by most measures of sensory and cognitive development. It seems that at birth, females demonstrate greater *interhemispheric connectivity* (Baron-Cohen, Lutchmaya, and Knickmeyer 2005), which suggests that, when compared to men, women's cerebral hemispheres "may communicate with each other to a greater degree" (Friedman and Downey 2008, p. 157). Might this have something to do with the fact that, at one day old, most infant girls prefer a live face while most boys choose a mechanical face? Could this be why girl babies tend to be slightly more socially attuned? Similarly, might there be different ways of managing relationships such that girl children are better at "empathizing" or striving to identify and respond appropriately to another's emotional state, while boys are better at relating by assessing the rules governing the interpersonal system or by "systematizing" (Baron-Cohen, Lutchmaya, and Knickmeyer 2005)?

The relationship between biology and the psychoanalytic approach to gender is quite apparent in research that suggests there is a psychophysiological component reflecting the infant male's *greater vulnerability to early neurobiological disruptions.* Thus, boys appear to have a greater need for a maternal object or caregiver to co-regulate, metabolize, and contain. For instance, the boy's frontal cortex, amygdala, and temporal lobe structuralization is slower, his recovery from elevated cortisol levels more prolonged, and language development is later (Baron-Cohen 2003; Martel et al. 2009; McClure 2000). Perhaps boys prior to age two require higher levels of parental input due to the slower pace of neurobiological development resulting from greater testosterone exposure in utero (Bertrand and Pan 2013).

Additional findings converge to suggest that boys are more limited in their ability to adjust to adversity before and after birth (Sandman, Glynn, and Davis 2013). Likewise, from birth to age two, boys who suffer from psychosocial deprivation are more vulnerable to disruptions of attachment (Drury et al. 2012; Kochanska, Coy, and Murray 2001; Zeanah et al. 2009). For example, when their mothers withdraw, three-month-old and six-month-old infant boys become more agitated than girls, require more time to return to normal interaction, and are more vulnerable to, as well as less resilient to, maternal depression (Martel et al. 2009; Tronick and Weinberg 2000; Weinberg et al. 1999; Weinberg et al. 2006). These early difficulties are subsequently manifest in greater externalizing and harmful acting-out behaviors (Fearon et al. 2010; Sroufe et al. 2005).

Of course, by citing data from the realm of neuroscience, I am moving beyond the purely psychoanalytic order—yet, I believe such findings are useful in discerning the role that gender may play within psychoanalytic space. Though research is in its early stages, even differences between males' and females' prenatal hormones and gender-based epigenetic responses to pre- and postnatal environments (Cortes, Cistemas, and Forger 2019), as well as their brains' sexual differentiations, have far-reaching effects on conscious and unconscious experience. These influences impact the experience of gender and sexuality that manifests in sex-linked play styles, toy preferences, fantasy life, and sex drive, as well as sexuality itself (Friedman and Downey 2008; see also Mayer 1991).

I consider next how the aforementioned cultural and biological factors intersect with psychodynamics to impact the male's construction of his internal sense of maleness.

The male ego ideal: influences from culture, anatomy, and psychodynamics

The metapsychological concept of *the ego ideal* seems particularly useful in assessing the influences of sociocultural and biological factors on the individual male's psychodynamics with respect to his masculine gender identity. I aim to make this clearer by returning to the little boy growing up in Westernized, phallocentric cultures.

Distinctive features of the male ego ideal

How can we understand the shaping of the boy's ego ideal along gendered lines? To put it more colloquially, why is the "male ego" so important for men? As explicated in Chapters 3 and 5, the gendered nature of the masculine ego ideal is founded on the boy's distinctive struggle during the initial stages of gender differentiation—a struggle requiring the little boy to adapt to a significant disruption in relation to his mother. It is the boy's gendered ego ideal that helps him heal what he experiences as an abrupt, rather traumatic sense of loss during his efforts to separate from her (Fast 1984, 1994).

Consequently, the boy's *phallic narcissism* helps defend against the terrifying annihilation dangers associated with his unrepresentable, primal, bodily based vulnerability that, like Achilles's heel, signifies the fragility of mortality, as well as the budding anxieties related to castration. These phallic and subsequent genital ego ideals reflect individually constructed fantasies that shape masculine gender identity in both healthy and pathological ways.

The boy's primary schema of connection is developed within attuned mother-son mutuality and provides him with a core sense of narcissistic cohesion. This core will have been internalized in the form of his earliest identification with and by his mother and thus continues to play an active intrapsychic role throughout life. However, I maintain that the boy *inevitably* experiences a gender-related, particularly forceful *traumatic* sense of loss during this early phase of separation-individuation, regardless of the severity and intensity of his struggle to separate from his mother (Diamond 1997, 2004b).[6] The basis for the inevitability of this traumatic loss lies in the fact that many of the traits and activities that culturally comprise gender identity can be traced to a process of unresolved mourning for cross-gender dependencies and identifications; early homoerotic attachments, particularly for the proto-gay boy whose father becomes rejecting in response to his son's gender nonconformity; and accompanying gender-inconsistent traits, particularly those that are coded by the boy/male culture as "feminine," including the receptive, relational, and emotional facets of intimacy. This societal form of gender imposition is frequently manifest as a deep but ungrievable loss with profound consequences (Butler 1995).

I call upon the familiar psychoanalytic notion of the ego ideal in order to explicate the nature of the male's struggle to heal the abrupt, traumatic loss of omnipotence that results from his early separation from his mother. As I've indicated in Chapter 3, because he must simultaneously recognize that he is *sexually different* from his mother just when he is *losing* her, the trauma is often shattering for the young boy because it reflects both the *lost dyadic connection* and the *narcissistic wound* subsequently caused by the culturally pressured repudiation of what was lost. The "double whammy" created by these twofold losses renders the boy's situation particularly wounding and therefore more developmentally challenging (Fast 1994, 1995). Regardless, the boy's trauma must be appreciated as a necessary loss that itself provides maturational opportunities.

The maturing male ego ideal

The man who is able to develop a maturing ego ideal that integrates the phallic ego ideal with the genital ego ideal (represented by the internalized, involved, and loving genital father) is freed from reliance on the bifurcated, phallicized manhood that plays such an important and beneficial role in his childhood, adolescent, and young adult adaptations. Thus, the achievement of a mature sense of masculine identity is dependent on the adequate negotiation of a shifting balance between the phallic ego ideal and the genital ego ideal throughout the life cycle.

For example, in early adulthood, men attempt to live up to idealized notions of what it is to be a man, and young adult men are typically dominated by the phallic ego ideal characterized by the *heroic illusion* (Levinson et al. 1978). Nonetheless, they must increasingly invoke a more genital ego ideal in striving to establish lasting, intimate relationships. If all goes well enough, there is an increased reality orientation; grandiosity lessens, a sense of otherness and empathy increases, and maturing adulthood is on course.

Yet, early maternal identifications remain significant in male psychic structure and typically come to play a more active role—and hopefully a more conscious one—as a man matures. In fact, a maturing gender identity develops from integrating early preoedipal identifications with both parents; this inevitably demands a noteworthy psychic achievement in the integrative-synthetic sphere. The establishment of gender identity begins, then, with the child's "capacity to identify with both mother and father at the same time" (Christiansen 1996, p. 113), while its eventual transformation requires what Thomas Ogden referred to as "the creation of a dialectical interplay between masculine and feminine identities" (1989, p. 138). A healthy, cohesive sense of manhood can evolve when *core gender identity* is not split off from a flexibly masculine *gender role identity*.

In short, gender role identity reflects an evolving dialectic between cohesiveness and fluidity. The *holding* frame of gender role identity, then, can bear the more ambiguous, contrasting, paradoxical, and conflicting aspects of one's multiple gender identifications. Perhaps this complexity is best captured in the poetic description of Ivan Illich, who characterized gender as "an ambiguous, asymmetrical dance" (cited in Diamond 1997, p. 450n).

In attaining this more differentiated *genital ego ideal*, issues pertaining both to the acceptance of the limitations of one's gender and to its contrasting elements no longer have to be denied in the service of primary narcissism. The man who has reached this level of psychic maturation does not have to have or be everything in order to experience his manhood with all its "limitations" (Fast 1984). Similarly, the previously renounced, overly inclusive opposite-sex identifications that were deemed gender inappropriate are reclaimable; antagonistic, contrasexual elements can be reunited (Bassin 1996; Elise 1998, 2001; Young-Eisendrath 1997). This maturational accomplishment is founded on developing the capacity for postconventional thought, whereby gendered opposites do not remain bifurcated but are instead "held" and symbolically bridged (Benjamin 1996).

I have tried to make clear in Chapter 3 that the old notion that femaleness must be overcome in order to create male development simply does *not* fit with the diverse gender identity narratives that our male patients present to us. Instead, an individual's fixed gender portrait, such as masculine/active/dominant or feminine/passive/submissive, essentially represents a defensive solution to the struggle involved in establishing gender identity (Balsam 2001). In essence, then, the "lived ambiguities of gender" (Benjamin 1996, p. 36) are tolerable only when this higher level of postoedipal differentiation is achieved by means of sustaining tension between contrasting elements that remain *available* rather than *forbidden*.

Developmental achievements in the areas of work, intimacy, and fathering or mentoring typically precede the impact of aging in stimulating the reshaping of the masculine ego ideal. The maturing man's task, then, is to integrate the various prephallic, phallic, and genital aspects of his inner world in order to achieve what might be termed the mature or "true" genital position, or genital masculinity, wherein phallic propensities are used in the service of reality. Kleinians emphasize the achievement of the depressive position through such attenuation of omnipotence and the importance of mourning (as seen with Raymond, the case discussed later in this chapter), and the maturing man is forced to deal with the "necessity of growing small" (Manninen 1992, p. 23) in order to become whole—less grandiose, omnipotent, phallic.[7] As a result, the ego ideal can become less sharply gendered, a more balanced yet fluid masculinity is attained, and the ideals previously associated with becoming a man give way to those associated with becoming a person.

Masculinity nonetheless persists in remaining tenuous; it does not simply progress in a linear way, nor does it necessarily manifest normativity. In short, *masculinity always involves loss, lack, and lifelong conflicts, tensions, and challenges pertaining to gendered ego ideals.* Instead of a primary resort to foreclosing, evacuative, or idealizing means to deal with these tensions, masculine progression requires the capacity to hold and contain the inherent strain of the irreducible predicament and intangibility that emerge from a man's shifting, coexisting prephallic, phallic, and genital positions. As I will explicate in Chapter 7 and in the book's concluding chapter (Chapter 8), this can result in a more flexible, fluid sense of gender identity—a maleness that truly incorporates what includes, in the language of the cultural binary, access to both the masculine and the feminine in the psyche. This reflects the man's development from residing mainly in the phallic position to achieving more of a genital ego ideal.

The following short vignette illustrates an adult patient's progression along these lines in the context of particular sociocultural and family influences on his psychodynamic structures. The patient relates a dream suggestive of a shift from the dyadic order to a triadic, more symbolic mode that enables changes in his ego ideal, so that it can progress from a phallic to a more *genital* position in which concern and mourning are sustained.

The case of Raymond: progression to a more genital position[8]

Raymond, an African American in his mid-thirties, began treatment following an incident of physically abusing his wife, from whom he was now separated. He was depressed, remorseful, and feared destroying his marriage to "the best woman I've ever known." Moreover, occasional episodes of alcohol and drug abuse threatened his career, causing him to worry that, like his father, he'd "make shit out of everything worthwhile."

His alcoholic father had abandoned Raymond and his infant twin brothers to his "loving but very doting" mother's care when he was six. At present, though he "hung out with many coworkers," Raymond had enormous difficulty relying on other men unless they were joined together to "defeat another organization." His transference to me was marked initially by a charming veneer barely disguising his considerable distrust. Once our racial differences and his concerns about me as a "White man" were discussed, our work could begin to explore Raymond's deeper transferences and dynamics reflecting his sense of oedipal "conquest" and accompanying failure to establish triangular relations—much like the psychic pictures of Charles and Jake, the men described in Chapter 5. "She was like my wife in a way," Raymond said in describing his mother, "and I was her 'special dude' who helped her raise the twins."

Raymond brought in a dream during our second year that depicted his longing for a *genital father* connected to his mother—a *triadic father*, representing a *genital ego ideal*, with whom he could identify and yet be generationally junior to. In the dream, Raymond was a teenager playing basketball on his driveway with his much-revered high school coach. They were playing *one on one* intensely when Raymond elbowed the older man away from guarding him. His elbow hit the coach's face, and blood began pouring out. The coach dropped to the ground "like a wounded bear," and Raymond was stunned and frightened. His mother had been watching, and she ran straight to the bleeding coach, ministering to him. She looked toward Raymond as if to say, "I love the coach like a husband, and I will take care of him even if you are scared."

Raymond awoke feeling strangely upset yet relieved. This relief suggests that he was searching for a mature, stable, and good enough oedipal father so that he would no longer be so plagued by the unconscious burden of being the *child-father*, with its accompanying sense of oedipal victory and excessive guilt. In the ensuing sessions, the necessary, albeit missing symbolic father functioning was becoming activated in our analytic relationship. Raymond indicated a change in his feelings about his attachment to me, and he began more openly to share his conflicts in the realm of sexuality and intimacy, as well as the shame that dwelled beneath his addictive escapes and the violent rage serving to preserve his fragile, rigidly held masculinity.

Brief case discussion

The dream suggests Raymond's oedipal-level movement in which his more exclusive, dyadic (and phallic-level) link to his mother (and wife) began to break up and shift to a triadic mode that enabled him to begin to bear his sense of loss and limitation. His concern for those whom he had damaged indicates an emergent depressive position that signals changes in his adult ego ideal, making clear his realistic needs for comfort and his compassion for others. Our work became increasingly marked by his sadness and regret for the ways in which he had hurt his wife and damaged other relationships with little preoccupation.

Despite his wife's divorcing him, we continued to meet for nearly two more years. We witnessed some rather remarkable shifts in Raymond's way of experiencing his masculinity as his ego ideal progressed from a phallic to a more genital position. He was becoming more capable of self-reflecting, of admitting limitations, and yet was actively and rather audaciously making use of his considerable strengths and resources to help him authentically bear his guilt, manage his addictive impulses, and mourn the end of his marriage.

Notes

1 In traditional developmental psychoanalysis, as noted in Chapters 1 and 2, the *core gender identity* of being either female or male is tied to the bedrock of anatomy and is thought to be established at birth through biology, sex assignment, and parental attitudes and behaviors. *Gender identity* itself—the felt sense of being feminine or masculine—represents an awareness of belonging to one sex and not the other (Stoller 1968).

2 As I've indicated, gender identity is complex and multifaceted for all males; moreover, gay and bisexual males struggle with their sense of maleness just as straight males do. The particular developmental pathway for any male—whether growing up in a traditional family or in a nontraditional interpersonal environment—remains unique and highly individualized. Nonetheless, proto-gay boys typically grow up as "outsiders" (just as do many sons of gay parents); consequently, forging a sense of maleness may entail additional trauma pertaining to being different from the cisgendered heterosexual order. (I.e., the experience tends to go beyond simply *being different from* the *mother's gender* and subsequently *feeling individuated from* her.) The extent of this third trauma suffered by the gay boy depends on the parenting couple's capacity to recognize and help metabolize his ensuing developmental issues. Though an in-depth exploration of these factors is beyond this book's purview, several important psychoanalytic works address the gender-related issues of gay males that have important implications for psychoanalytic treatment. In particular, I strongly recommend the

seminal writings of Kenneth Lewes (1988), Richard Isay (1989), Martin Frommer (1994, 2000), and Sidney Phillips (2001, 2004). Moreover, a thoughtful consideration of a father's impact on a gay boy, whose difference can mark the boy as an *abject other,* is offered by Seidman and Frank (2019).

3 In an effort to transcend psychoanalysis's binary perspective on femininity, German analyst Ilka Quindeau (2013) challenges both the *classical psychoanalytic* view of femininity as deviation from the masculine, signifying deficit and lack, and the *feminist-oriented, differentiating* view of positive femininity. Instead, she offers a third view, one that entails an inherent, ever-present gender conflict wherein fluidity and fixity resulting from innate, biologically essential facets are held in tension with socially constructed ones. Along Laplanchian lines (also suggested by Dio Bleichmar [1995], Harris [2005], and Diamond [2015]), gender is taken to be plural rather than binary. However, today, when theorizing in this realm of the binary—and despite the fact that the feminine has emerged from the view of woman as *the other* (rather than conceived solely out of otherness; see Glocer Fiorini 2007, 2017), the feminine, even for the male, is more aptly reconsidered in terms of *diversity* or *difference.*

4 Much of the evidence for this was garnered three decades ago (e.g., Betcher and Pollack 1993; Ehrensaft 1987), well before the broad shifts in the gender landscape characterized by an increasing normalization of multi-genderedness, changing gender roles, and post-traditional families that often de-genderize parenting (Seidman and Frank 2019). I am not aware of data from recent generations pertaining to the psychodynamics of boys' gender identity formations (including psychic representations for millennials). I suggest, however, that it is still too early to speculate about how psychic representations of mothers and fathers will differ among children of single parents and those of homosexual parents, as the gender arrangements of parenting and the complexities of gender continue to shift over current and future generations.

5 Although I do not discuss transgender or transsexual patients in this book, analysts such as Alessandra Lemma (2013, 2018), who works extensively with trans patients, remind us that such formulations are at the "intersection of sociocultural processes and individual psychodynamics" (2018, p. 1092). Moreover, the fantasies about and relationship to one's body remain central while posing many challenges for the analyst—and this is particularly so for those of us more steeped in conventional, binary ideas pertaining to gender.

6 As noted in the previous section, the boy's loss is especially traumatic for several reasons. In particular, boys are more reliant on their (typically) maternal caregivers for help with their emotional regulation and are more reactive to maternal emotions; hence, they seem to be at greater risk of suffering from traumatic caregiving environments, such as with depressed mothers (Tronick and Reck 2009). This results in a genderization of the relationship between boys and their mothers—that is, an especially *genderized system of relating* (Sroufe et al. 2005)—that impacts boys (and later men) in particular ways.

7 Manninen's poetic metaphor evidences that we need not rely on metapsychological constructs to appreciate what is involved in the maturation of the sense of maleness (or, in more formal terms, the construction and consolidation of adult masculine gender identity).

8 The case of Raymond has been previously discussed (Diamond 2007).

7 Maturing masculinity, receptivity, and gender fluidity: its trajectory through midlife transitions and later life changes

In this chapter, one of this book's key topics—viewing male gender identity as a *developmental trajectory*, rather than as inborn and static—is discussed in depth. The concept of the *male ego ideal* and its changing scope over time is examined, along with the value of healthy masculine sexuality in all its facets. In striving to achieve the ego ideal, a man gains access to receptivity and other so-called typically feminine traits residing deep within the male interior. These traits are present from the onset of life as what I term the *proto-genital masculine essence*, which I describe as a basic aspect of the genital position. Through accessing this interiorized realm whereby inside and outside are linked in relationship, gender fluidity in the psyche—*psychic bigenderality*—increases, which contributes significantly to maturing masculinity. Also in this chapter, I explore the particular challenges and developmental opportunities faced by men in mid- and later life and how these impact their gender identity and sexuality. The applicability of these ideas is illustrated by a detailed clinical vignette describing the treatment of a man struggling with a depressive crisis in midlife.

Recognizing the psyche of the other

There's an old joke about what might have occurred in the Garden of Eden before God created Eve out of Adam's rib. In this less androcentric version, God creates Eve first and then tells her he will create a husband for her. "What's a husband?" Eve asks. God replies, "He's someone who can fight to protect you from enemies and who will hunt to help you acquire food to eat." Eve thinks that sounds pretty good, so she tells God that it's fine by her. "But," God adds, "one thing you must understand—*he's going to need to think he's first* so you will have to let him think that it is so!"

I suggest that this joke's wit connects deeply with something known more unconsciously. Consequently, I will attempt to clarify how and why such cognizance of the psyche of the other seems to more naturally reflect what we tend to think of as "feminine," and, as I propound in this chapter, it plays an important role in the male's attaining a maturing, genital ego ideal.

To express this idea in Freudian drive-based terms, the mature ego ideal is made manifest in the seeking of *instinctual discharge* combined with a *concern for the object.* This maturing sense of masculinity consequently requires the attenuation of childish narcissism and omnipotence, accompanied by the growth of a more healthy, *adaptive* narcissism (involving strength, power, and assertion). Also required is a more realistic adaptation to limitations, as well as an enhanced capacity for mature object relations in which individuality is experienced in dialectic with both *generativity* (Erikson 1950) and *otherness*. The appearance of such a mature, genital ego ideal is aptly described as "supplying love its daily bread" (Chasseguet-Smirgel 1985, p. 72).

Maturing ego ideals and male receptivity

Beginning in a boy's early childhood, the evolution toward greater *receptivity to otherness* is outside of and *beyond* the phallic position, with its more conventional binary coding of have/have not. Relinquishing phallic omnipotence requires facing both the loss of control over one's objects and the realistic limitations of one's gender, objects, and self. I propose that from the very onset of life, commencing with the male infant's prephallic helplessness and primordial vulnerability—what might be termed the *proto-genital masculine essence*—certain qualities exist beyond the penetrating, more boundaried, differentiating, and exterior ones associated with healthy phallicism. Contrary to what might be characterized as popular belief (at least in many cultures), the male infant has far more than we typically believe of what is conventionally considered feminine in his capacities for open, receptive, spatial, connecting, and interior aspects of psychic experience (Diamond 1998, 2006; Elise 2001; Fogel 1998; Friedman 1996; Kestenberg 1968). I will argue, however, that for many males, developing the ability to access this interiorized, proto-genital essence is not to be taken for granted; it remains a significant accomplishment.

As I've discussed in previous chapters, beginning at about two years of age, the little boy experiences visceral inner genital sensations during his initial gender crisis—sensations that are grounded in the inherent fraility of the infant's sucking to take in from the breast. This experience produces overwhelming floods of excitation in the boy that are inherently anxiety provoking, and are consequently defensively externalized as the boy associates the inside of the body with femininity (Kestenberg 1968). These inner sensations bear directly on the primordial vulnerability at the heart of the male psyche, as the boy's wishes to be penetrated are projected onto women and subsequently onto homosexual and "girlie" men.

In order for the boy to accept and reclaim his inner genital experiences during this phase, the link between his insides and his mother—and/or the feminine—must be attenuated. Once that occurs, the oft-neglected importance of the male's unconscious longing to embrace the receptivity, yielding, and surrender associated with the vagina and womb as an inner productive space to be penetrated and known—his desire for, as well as his envy of, the womb or vagina (Boehm 1930; see also Elise 2001)—can take its rightful place alongside both *breast envy* and *penis envy* as fundamental organizing experiences in male psychic development, as the developing boy becomes better able to overcome his terrors of the inside as dangerous.

The culturally specific minimization of this more interiorized dimension of masculinity—his *inner genitality*—undoubtedly has something to do with penetration anxieties. For instance, Elise (2001) advocates that the masculine sense of self, at least in adult, heterosexual males, is dependent upon an impermeable psychic boundary termed the *citadel complex,* which is not to be penetrated (since being penetrated is equivalent to femininity). Accordingly, adult male development requires working through the "fear of having a 'womb'—an inner productive space, an internal space that can be penetrated and known—where something about the private self can be discovered and revealed" (ibid., p. 501).

Friedman (1996) reasoned similarly that post-phallic-stage males deny their inner body and testicles. To attain what I denote as the genital ego ideal, he emphasized the need to recognize more of the male's anxieties pertaining to repudiated "inner space" (partially represented by the testicles), which in turn tends to be projected onto women. In contrast, then, the phallic male's denial of the inside "dark continent" of his inner body produces a defensive focus on the external body and on mastery of the external world—part of an exaggerated *phallic identity.* This is often manifest in a heightened reliance on the thinking apparatus or on external action, while having less access to the deeper, more bodily based realms of feeling and specific anxieties about what is "hanging out" there.

Thus, the more traditional representation of male sexuality as purely phallic, with interiority ignored (e.g., that is embodied by the testicles), can be viewed as a defensive distortion (Elise 2001; Fogel 1998; Friedman 1996). This reliance on defensive phallicism in adulthood is characterized as a "hardening of the heart" that protects men from the "dangers of exposing softer and more tender inner organs and psychical sensibilities" (Fogel 1998, p. 679).

Nonetheless, as I examined in Chapter 2, adjacent to phallic demarcation and delinking is an openness and receptivity to the other that the cultural world speciously circumscribes as the differentiated province of the female. In his accessing this openness and receptivity to the other, the man in the genital position utilizes the capacity for binding together and attaching equal importance to his own and his partner's satisfaction, both bodily and psychologically. This reflects both whole-object relating and object concern indicative of the Kleinian depressive position (with attendant anxieties pertaining to guilt for damaging the loved object). Thus, the penis contra the phallus in genital sexuality operates as an instrument of both Eros and linkage—indicating a *going inside of* another (Bion 1959).

From the position of the genital ego ideal, the penis is primarily an object for relations and connection, wherein the penis-as-link promotes mental space and thinking (Birksted-Breen 1996). In its recognition of the parental couple and mental bisexuality, the penis has a structuring function, at least within Freudian dual-drive theorizing, as an instrument of Eros—in contrast to the phallus as an instrument of Thanatos, one that aims to destroy such linkings. Hence, "the *maternal function* of being with and the *paternal function* of ... linking" are combined (ibid., p. 652, italics added).

Besides reflecting receptivity and passivity, however, the inner genital also encompasses an active, aggressive component most evident in incorporative impulses, with their anal-sadistic features (Chasseguet-Smirgel 1964). In this respect, the ineradicable sexual binary of receptivity/penetrability, as well as an unsealable psychic sexual opening in the male's mode of receptivity, implies moving outside the spurious gender binary and the phallic world of quantity. Through transcending residence in the phallic position, the man experiences an expansion of bodily sensual pleasure beyond the satisfactions associated with the penis, including the enjoyment of both a wider range of visceral excitation and increased procreative space during ejaculation.[1]

Genital primacy, or *genital love,* a far more complicated notion than mere genital potency, combines genital satisfaction with pregenital tenderness (Balint 1948), a psychic feat permitting receptivity to otherness that requires the male to access his own vulnerability—his Achilles heel. Thus, becoming and being a man, in addition to penetration and creativity, is marked by *absence* and elements of *lack, loss,* and "an enduring experience of *deficiency*" (Moss 2012, p. 34, italics added). Achieving this ultimate genital organization in which inside and outside—body, psyche, and external world—are linked in active relationship to one another is considered essential for a successful psychoanalysis (Balint 1950; see also Freud 1937).

Healthy masculine sexuality

Maturing, healthy genitality is characterized by the attenuation of anxieties pertaining both to masculine inner space and to non-penis-dominated sensuality, as well as the lessening of anxieties associated with their psychic sensibilities related to experiences of limitation and need. By conditionally accepting his insides, the male finds that a receptive mental space for passive surrender is provided, as well as the ability to *identify with* rather than *repudiate* the feminine (Kestenberg 1968). This postambivalent integration of phallic propensities in the service of reality, characterized by penetration and receptivity, is founded on Eros, which aims for connection.

As discussed in Chapters 2 and 3, the term *genitality*, particularly when operative in the sexual sphere, involves adaptive assertion, aggression, and modulated phallicism, in which penetration in the service of mastery, potency, and authority are integrated with more receptive needs for connection and attachment. Phallic urges are present and remain significant, but in their genital countenance are transformed into more aim-inhibited and object-recognizing forms. In this respect, there is a strong resemblance between the analytic ideal of the genital character and both the Anglo-Saxon prototype of a gentleman and the Judeo-Hebraic exemplar of a *mensch*. Speaking psychosexually, the maturing man's genital features help him become oriented more toward making love than simply fucking—though of course the impulse to fuck re-mains an important dimension of his masculinity and lovemaking.

As the genital ego ideal strengthens, both the *hierarchical* (high/low, big/ little) and the *relational* (linking) facets of maleness become part of a com-plex yet more flexible psychic structure, which no longer rigidly defends against emasculation by retreating from those aspects of psychic reality found most threatening, including what may well be the most durable characteristic of masculinity (as well as of femininity)—namely, its containment of un-symbolizable, primordial vulnerability. Nonetheless, enduring unconscious resistances to giving over to something beyond the self—necessitated in dif-ferentiating from the maternal object—often impede actual intercourse with a loved partner; for example, in the *Madonna/whore complex,* wherein the "affectionate" and "sensual" currents are kept apart (Freud 1912), as evident with Charles, the case discussed in Chapter 5.

In contrast, when (seminal) linking does occur, a less conflicted, un-conscious embracing of receptivity partially erases the gender binary for ei-ther the gay or straight man who, like his mother before him when suckling her infant, gives to an other from within. Masculine gender can consolidate in such a flexible manner, then, only when phallicism ceases to dominate, and when genitality, with its more optimal, fluid, and complex sense of gender differentiation and multiplicity, takes on its rightful place in the psyche (Aron 1995; Bassin 1996; Fast 1984, 1990). As the vicissitudes of phallic narcis-sism, with its ubiquitous grandiose illusions, attenuate through integration and mastery, culturally sanctioned ideals of manhood, reflective of culturally shared components of the adult male's genital ego ideal, can become realized.

Psychic structures change during the life cycle process and are marked by ego regressions and reorganizations (Erikson 1950). I will consider next the kinds of likely opportunities and challenges that occur as the male adult ego ideal shifts over the course of life.

Transformations as the man moves through life

In essence, then, the male ego ideal typically becomes less sharply gendered as he matures, particularly during midlife, as the middle-aged man seeks to recover early internal objects that had to be foreclosed in his adaptive and often more manic efforts to achieve a stable sense of self and gender identity. For most men in the Western world—as for Alan, the patient I will discuss later in this chapter—the reorganizational process usually involves redis-covering the feminine, those contrasexual objects representing the mysterious "darkness" that Freud alluded to (i.e., male interiority, which Jungians term the *shadow*). In contrast, however, for many men in the artistic, educational, mental health, and healing professions—as well as men trapped in what traditional Freudians have depicted as the *negative Oedipus,* and perhaps those suffering from what Ken Corbett (2009) more recently termed *phal-lophobia*—it is not uncommon to observe that the midlife descent often involves re-accessing what may be more conventionally considered masculine representations that had been radically sublimated, foreclosed, or disavowed. I refer here specifically to components of competitiveness, phallic aggression, carnal sexuality, and masculine forms of destructiveness. For these less conventional men, the midlife reworking of the depressive position often strengthens the capacity to accept and tolerate conflict, ambivalence, and destructiveness in both their adaptive and pathological forms. Thus, for both more "traditional" men and less typical ones, ideals previously associated with becoming a man give way to those associated with becoming a person, and "the normal unisex of later life" emerges (Gutmann 1964).

As noted in Chapter 2, a healthy sense of masculine gender identity involves an ongoing process spanning pivotal stages throughout a man's life. The midlife task in regard to masculinity entails renewing an acquaintance with previously rejected gendered dimensions of the self—particularly many of the male individual's early identifications and internalized objects that had been set aside because of their seeming incompatibility with his more constricted, rigidly ossified, phallic sense of masculinity, a feature that may have been necessary during adolescence and early adulthood.

During this phase, the man's divergent identifications can be adaptively and more flexibly activated, and as I've noted, the pleasures of receptivity, being, experiencing, and understanding frequently come to take precedence over the excitement of striving and reaching, while priority is given to insight, connection, and nurturance. Midlife offers unique possibilities for such transformations for those men who have relied on more defensively phallic, less pluralistic constructions of their internal, subjective sense of masculinity. Midlife individuation, the so-called *fourth individuation,* consequently takes place through attempts to come to terms with those parts of himself that were disowned largely out of fear of being deprived of masculine gender identity (Colarusso 1997). By and large, then, the middle-aged man must make room within for the internal feminine to animate him as his biological fires dwindle (Jung 1934).

Challenges and opportunities for the aging man

The aging man, like Hermes guiding souls to the Underworld, is thus called upon to accept the need for going downward or inward to bring to light those parts of himself previously disowned. This *regression in the service of ego development* furthers his integration of the darker, more obscure, and mysterious sides of himself, as well as his softer and more yielding aspects, rendering his maturing life's quest less discordant. A more balanced yet fluid masculinity is achieved.

To reiterate, then, and to emphasize a key point, the challenge for the aging man necessitates coming to terms with parts of his psyche that were necessarily renounced or repudiated earlier in order to establish a stable sense of identity. There is an awakening during what we might think of as life's second half, perhaps related to physiological changes, in which the psyche becomes engaged in a process of descent—a propelling inward and down-ward in order to experience a sense of meaning beyond the mere facts of physical existence. This often entails upgrading ways of "being that [were] previously experienced as 'feminine'" (Labouvie-Vief 1994, p. 18).

Many men come to recognize their gendered complexity during the crucial separations/individuations of early adulthood (Colarusso 2000). However, in midlife, owing to the ultimate bodily basis of the experience of gender, a man's sense of his changing masculinity can often serve to weight the perpetual male struggle along genital lines, both in the more tradi-tionally represented exterior sense and, as noted earlier in this chapter, in the less examined interior manner. Consequently, a transformed masculi-nity subsequently becomes evident in a man's increasing capacity for a more fluid yet complexly gendered experience.

There are multiple biological and psychological (along with social) de-terminants of this crucial transition as one first begins to deal with loss of youth, tries to match the percept of an aging self with the memory of a younger self, begins to perceive the passage of time differently, and relates more per-sonally to death, with the accompanying realization of a finite amount of time left. For most men, by the age of forty-five, the adaptive, "pressured man-hood" (Gilmore 1990), arising from the young man's efforts to prove his manliness, begins to attenuate. Moreover, the normative grandiosity of early adulthood lessens, and the individual must confront his shortcomings and destructiveness, along with the awareness that he, too, will die (Jacques 1965).

The next phase of life, signaled by confrontation with one's personal death and its attendant anxieties, optimally leads to further transformations of the male ego, especially in the decline of phallic masculinity. There is a new set of tasks pertaining less to establishing one's sense of identity in the world and more to the need for meaning. To reiterate, parts of the psyche that were necessarily renounced or repudiated previously in order to establish a stable sense of identity are awakened, and priority is often given to insight and nurturance, perhaps related to the diminishment of testosterone.[2]

Thus, the man in midlife is given an opportunity to transform his gender identity by developing his capacity to contain the tension that is inherent between his core sense of who he is and the fundamentally fluid, shifting nature of his multifaceted self (Bromberg 1998). In fact, gender identity may be the arena in which the aging man experiences the most radical deconstruction of his male certitude as he experiences a shifting from his more action-oriented modes to a more inward, integrative perspective, embracing the lost parts of the self. More manic defenses that served to cut off awareness of inner psychic reality can attenuate as arrival at the hum-bling, depressive crossroads of midlife enables the necessary mourning to ensue, along with the reestablishment of renounced, lost childhood objects.

As I've noted, however, development is arrested when the maturing man continues to call upon defensive phallicity to maintain his sense of masculinity, and when he persists in defining himself by conquest and aggression within hierarchical-based relations. We see this all too often in the sad efforts of many men who tear apart their lives and families to attain a "trophy wife," or in their ruthless pursuit of achievement on various levels until their bodies simply grind to a halt. These are the aging men who keep trying to prove their manhood, when—primarily through their more conscious relational needs—they would be better served by embracing their personhood.

Later-life masculinity

As men move beyond middle age, losses related to aging mount, particularly with respect to physical changes. Consequently, a man's opportunities for ongoing later-life development depend upon his healthy midlife gender identity integration, as well as on his capacity both for generativity and successful mourning.

With respect to later-life gender identity, potential mortifications and narcissistic crises characterized by shame, indignity, and humiliation may occur as a result of the challenges inherent to acknowledging physical disintegration, separation and loss, dependency, and the inevitability of time as a pervasive fact of life. Indeed, fantasies of omnipotence are at least severely challenged, if not brought to a complete halt. The reality of old age forces one to give up the fantasies of undying objects and to abandon the hunt for an ideal object (Schafer 1968). Manic, phallic-narcissistic defense mechanisms tend to lose their power, and growing acceptance replaces the manic search for the ideal.

Old age becomes particularly mortifying for men whose gender identity tends to remain distinctively phallic and narcissistic (Teising 2008). In these cases, the illusory venture of the phallic conquest of the world may be pursued up to the end of life, and feelings of helplessness, need, and despair are disavowed—while grandiose, omnipotent fantasies and actions attempt to preserve the illusion of control over the fundamentally out-of-control nature of aging and dying. As I will present in the next section, the case of Alan suggests that the successful transformation of the phallic-narcissistic elements of the male ego ideal during midlife helps establish the elderly male's later-life course. Regardless, later life provides an additional opportunity for achieving a more integrated gendered identity; for example, parent-child roles are typically reversed as the old become dependent on the care provided by the young (Diamond 2007).

For the aging man, physical frailty and dependence, as well as the inevitability of death, are more easily acknowledged when he can integrate into his own identity the requirement to receive care—or, as Martin Teising describes it, "an internal space representing the female—formerly experienced within the maternal other" (2007, p. 1337). This may reflect the realization of increased gender fluidity in which the psyche's essential bigenderality is more fully embraced. Moreover, as discussed in Chapters 4 and 5 in relation to the formation of the genital object, this comforting and containing internal object is initially most likely to develop from the care provided by an attuned mother, as well as by an involved and loving father (or surrogate). A comforting, caring internal object is therefore available when external objects are lost, and so can help provide sufficient containment within relationships as the elderly man attempts to master the crisis of physical aging.

The case of Alan: a concealed search for the "lost father of interiority"[3]

Alan, a 43-year-old, married father of two young boys, began treatment describing his unhappiness due to his wife's "volatility and moodiness." He asked if I could help him figure out what he might do so that "she" wouldn't be so irritable, depressed, and angry. About to undergo major knee surgery, Alan was distressed about his body "starting to fail." Like many men at midlife, he felt that he had "climbed the mountain of success" and was no longer so anxiously driven about work. His considerable career and financial successes had been expedited by his well-developed, phallic masculinity. In addition to enabling him to adaptively penetrate the outer world, this brand of masculinity also served as a fulcrum for an obsessive, hypomanic exterior orientation that warded off depressive anxieties. At the onset of treatment, however, the situation with his wife began to occupy center stage, and it gradually became clear that beyond Alan's scaled "mountain" lay a darker, more ominous valley of the unknown that threatened to engulf him.

Alan's depressive anxieties gradually became analyzable as he spoke of being fearful of getting lost in a disturbing world of feelings about his life circumstances. He feared being once again left alone prematurely with no one to help him traverse what he termed "the wide unknown" (i.e., the more spatial, less contoured, and ambiguous realms of his emotionally dominated interior world). Alan was partially drawn to an analysis in which I re-presented a Poseidon-like father personifying power in the realm of instinct and emotion. At the same time, however, his efforts at affect modulation seemed doomed as he feared that his analyst (myself as his Poseidon-father) would leave him long before he could successively contain (rather than cut off) and creatively express his potentially disruptive emotions.

Alan was filled with anxiety and shame about being drawn into his internal world. For him, that ambiguous world of feelings, contours, and spatiality was problematic precisely because it lacked sharply distinct borders and certitude. As I will explicate, his use of externalizing, phallic masculine defenses in the form of manic activity and obsessive (non)thinking can be understood in terms of his reliance on a rigid, constricted form of masculine gender identity, one characterized by an insufficiently internalized genital father.

Alan was the only child of an aloof yet quite distinguished, scholarly professor and his much younger immigrant wife. His already-elderly father died when he was eight years old following a sudden, debilitating three-year illness that resulted in severe premature dementia. Although Alan would often become tearful when discussing his father's death, he regularly would add that he "took after" his father while remaining very close to his mother despite her "flakiness." Like his father, Alan was a highly educated man who prided himself on both his intellect and his physical prowess; he was an expert mountain climber as well as a highly successful intellectual.

Shortly after beginning treatment, Alan expressed considerable confusion as to what he was "supposed to do" and what was "supposed to happen." Dismayed and perplexed, he contrasted the analysis with his recent knee surgery. He wished our work were more like surgery, "where I can trust my doctor to just put me to sleep and correct whatever damage there may be in my body." In contradistinction to the powerful surgeon (father) who could render him unconscious and repair damage, I initially represented a more powerless (mother-like) figure that stood for such nebulous things as "relationships" and "emotions," rather than the more highly valued, paternal qualities of "discovery" and "knowledge."

Alan was ashamed of his close ties with his mother, and in fact his wife, apparently threatened by their closeness, would angrily accuse him of having "an unnatural relationship" with his mother. Our discussions of such insinuations were punctuated by his highly charged, angry denials, and he fiercely let me know that "those psychoanalytic oedipal theories about mothers and sons are far-fetched." Alan's masculine gender identity was indeed maintained in a delicate narcissistic balance, and I had to tread carefully but straightforwardly in exploring the mother-son theme lest he experience me as similarly fearful of facing such shameful issues.

The first several years of the treatment process were marked by a clear sense of our making contact and then having it ruptured rather abruptly. This is illustrated by an episode during our tenth month when Alan became especially upset with the treatment, following a particularly emotional session in recalling his father's three-year decline and subsequent death. He had been ruminating about his unhappy marriage and couldn't see that "what we've been discussing has any value or is related to the 'real' problem." He explained that he had come to therapy in order to find a way to alter his wife's behavior toward him or, at the very least, to "find a better way to live with her." "What's the point of all this emotion, and how will it improve my marriage?" he asked repeatedly.

Indeed, I, too, began to wonder what "the point" might be, while noticing that I felt compelled to console him by providing "*the* answer." I struggled to contain my impulse to reduce both his anxieties and my own, stemming from what appeared to be a frightening chaos that was seemingly silenced only through authoritative cognition. I had to use my clinical experience in working with projective identification to recover my ability to verbalize an understanding of his fears of being left alone in the seemingly illogical terrain of feelings.

As I worked to contain Alan's terror of becoming enticed by and ultimately drowned in affective chaos, he began to cast himself as a man dying of thirst while his wife (and analyst) seemed to provide only a dry, empty well, depriving him of vital liquid (milk). I reflected on how upsetting our previous session had been for him and how hard he seemed to struggle to find a way to contain the "well spring" inside him. He became very quiet before sharing that this made him think of the deeply affecting film *Field of Dreams;* he said that he had found himself crying when the protagonist's deceased father returned to play catch with his grownup son. Alan longingly recalled how his own father played ball with him on those rare occasions when he was home and still healthy, and, just as Alan began to make this meaningful contact with himself, he quickly crushed it by accessing what we came to call his "technological focus."

His thoughts again turned to his marriage and his wife's "problems" to which he compulsively sought a solution. I felt left out in the cold, and on this occasion, partly as a result of recognizing my own feelings of abandonment in our contact with one another, I was able to help him address his defensive need to preserve his tenuous sense of masculinity that underlay the consuming focus on his wife. I explained that he seemed to abruptly disappear from his "feeling" self in a way that was similar to how he might have experienced his father's sudden demise. I proposed that he didn't want to show me how "thirsty" he was for his father because to do so would revive both his feelings of *fatherly loss* and his deep needs for his *mother's comfort.* He indicated that he recognized how often he felt ashamed to expose these basic feelings because he "might be seen as defective."

Alan eventually acknowledged how much he wanted to be recognized for simply "being a guy" among other males. For example, in reflecting on the pain he had often felt as a child on the playground, he declared, "I just wanted to be 'a guy-guy' and belong." His wife's idealizing admiration earlier in their relationship for his "special" manliness that included his sensitivity and kindness had only temporarily attenuated his core anxieties about his masculinity. As his marital difficulties mounted and his wife consistently devalued him as "just another typically selfish man," Alan began to reexperience the wounds associated with the lack of a genital paternal imago capable of validating his complex and multifaceted masculinity—a masculinity that could include the recognition and acceptance of his maternal identifications. Unable to optimally experience his own de-idealization, Alan began to relive the childhood humiliation when he "couldn't make it with the 'guy-guys.'"

Two distinct transference constellations became central well into our work. In one, I was the "flaky" *maternal object* representing a journey into the unbounded and messy, interior realm where contact might emerge from within the imprecisely shaped, less concrete contours and spatiality of the inner world of affect and imaginings. For instance, Alan would often question the value of discussing anything beyond the problems in his marriage. He assumed a position similar to that which he had come to believe that his father might have taken. He took on the role of a skeptic who would oppose his mother's (and analyst's) "unscientific" forays into what he teasingly called "touchy-feely" realms. An understanding of this transference (and my accompanying countertransference) helped in appreciating Alan's need to define himself as masculine by dint of a bifurcated, staunch opposition to a feared entrance into the "flaky" and "unscientific" feminine world. As we analyzed this, he began to realize the enormous psychic effort that he exerted in an attempt to create sharp, distinctive borders typically involving robust and sure cognition. He hoped this would protect him from being drawn into the more chaotic, less bounded interior world associated with his wife and mother.

In the second transference configuration, I became the needed *dyadic, paternal object* of genital interiority—a self-object that represented maleness both desiring and affirming of his masculinity (in the context of his existence in relation to his inner world and the interior realms equated with his mother). Meaningful work emerged from this transference, which helped Alan reaccess his lost internal father. In the homoerotic transference and countertransference dimensions, he began to experience loving feelings toward me while sensing the mutuality of my feelings toward him. He eventually experienced me as capable of containing his internal world and remaining with him while he mourned both the loss of his actual father and the foreclosure of so much of himself in an effort to erect a stable, albeit rigid and distinctly shaped structure for his masculinity. Immense sadness and grief arose as Alan began to reinternalize a paternal object—serving as a symbolic preoedipal and oedipal father that could desire his messy, unbounded self, so like his mother, while affirming his essential maleness via reciprocal identification.

A paternal imago was gradually established through the analytic relationship that was differentiated from the maternal world while still recognizing his need for connection. Alan came to understand that he had to create a "phallic" stance toward his interior life to conceal what he regarded as his inferior qualities linked to "femininity." His feared femininity actually reflected his intense longing to feel desired by a male presence that responded to his needs for masculine affirmation. He was ashamed of these needs and sought to obscure them in a rigid version of masculinity that subsumed the more phallic, knight-in-shining-armor qualities of the idealized father of his own construction and, most likely, those of his mother's construction. Alan clung tenaciously to a view of his "brilliant, witty, skeptical, and renowned" father—an academic knight, to be sure—in order to prevent his descent into those characteristics that he had incorrectly concluded to be *solely* the province of the feminine.

Brief case discussion

Alan's anxious, shame-dominated midlife crisis revealed the magnitude of his previous psychic restriction whereby his masculine identity was consolidated largely through mastery of external activity. As a result, the normative male midlife transition involving the creation of an alternative, middle-aged version of masculinity became instead a developmental crisis.

Its marker was the breakup of sharp, penetrating facets of his phallic exteriority, along with an increasingly disturbing access to his repressed interior world. The ensuing disruption was initially met by a defensive phallicity that served to ward off chaotic dangers that he associated with the less bounded, more spatial inner world of affect, impulse, and imagination.

Alan desperately needed both to reclaim the lost parts of his inner self and to come to terms with his limitations. His depressive and fragmentation anxieties led him into an analytic treatment that would help him achieve a more developed genitality encompassing greater gender fluidity (and bi-genderality) in which he relied less on gender splitting, while paradoxically further incorporating the interior realms of the masculine.

As the treatment progressed, Alan became more aware of his pivotal gender identity anxieties about "being a regular guy." He was increasingly able to internalize a genital paternal imago, both in its preoedipal and oedipal countenance, that incorporated the inward-directed, more open, and receptive dimensions of space and ambiguity, which served to establish deeper contact with both himself and the differentiated other. He no longer needed to repudiate his interior world of affect, need, and intense longing in order to feel desired by a male presence.

In coming to recognize the need for genital fathering, Alan found that his relationship to his now-latency-age son began to change. He developed the ability to contain his own disappointment regarding his son's lack of athleticism while supporting the boy's artistic interests, all the while continuing to mentor him in the realm of masterly pursuits. Alan could finally better understand and accept his own limitations while becoming content with something less than an idealized, narcissistic wholeness. The balance of forces was shifting such that a complex and fluid man, yet a more stable and mature one, could more comfortably feel a sense of (hu)manhood that was no longer so unconsciously gendered. Consequently, as a result of successfully reorganizing his ego ideal during midlife, he was better situated to handle the challenges of later life.

Notes

1 This is evident among both heterosexual and homosexual men who yearn not only for the pleasures of the penis-in-vagina and/or penis-in-anus, but also enjoy being penetrated, having the testicles or breasts stimulated, experiencing seminal ejaculation involving both retention and release, feeling pleasure through the use of the mouth, and fantasizing, as well as engaging in a variety of sexual practices that are too easily societally pathologized (Figlio 2010; Reis 2009; see also Boehm 1930).

2 There may be considerable intrapsychic turmoil associated with the renunciation of illusions and the acceptance of one's limitations intrinsic to this period. This can contribute to a sense of *ennui* and a sort of depressive crisis that reflects pain at having had to restrict oneself psychically in order to achieve sufficient mastery in the arena of external action (Jacques 1965). Nonetheless, this *constriction of*

the self produces a developmental need both to reclaim the lost parts of the self and to come to terms with one's limitations. Consequently, we often see a disengagement from the emotional impact of the environment during middle age (Auchincloss and Michels 1989), a growth of interiority (Pruyser 1987), greater receptivity to affiliative and nurturing urges (Neugarten 1968), and an effort to integrate the *internal feminine* and more consciously mediate between polarities (Jung 1934; Levinson et al. 1978).

3 Alan was previously discussed under a different name (Diamond 2004a).

8 Gender and masculinity in analytic practice, and concluding thoughts

My final chapter addresses how the psychoanalytic process can facilitate the male patient's new and more positive experience of masculinity. I discuss how an experiential and ideological broadening of the sense of maleness and gender, both for patients and their analysts, often requires working beyond phallic ego ideals and defenses as well as becoming more receptive to prephallic, primordial vulnerabilities in order to provide greater access to the receptive, so-called *feminine* interior. I emphasize the particular impact of the analyst and discuss the importance of the male analyst's incorporation of the feminine and gender fluidity. I close by summarizing the book's central themes—including the idea that masculinity always remains tenuous—and by adding some concluding thoughts.

Psychoanalysis and the opportunity for a new experience of masculinity

As illustrated by the cases of Seth, a young man in his twenties; Rich, a new father; Charles, a man trapped in the Madonna/whore complex; Raymond, a divorcing husband; and Alan, a man at midlife—the patients discussed in Chapters 2, 4, 5, 6, and 7, respectively—a new experience of masculinity is often achieved via the psychoanalytic treatment process. This results in an integration and synthesis of the more concrete, polarized images of holding and interpreting, receptivity and activity, and subjectivity and objectivity, as well as the analyst's ways of being, spontaneity, reflective awareness, and ability to make use of his/ her own reveries, subjectivity, and countertransference to further the analysis.

By reworking the relationship between the prephallic, phallic, and genital features of masculinity through the psychoanalytic treatment process or through life experience, many men achieve a new experience of their masculinity. The need for a clearly defined, well-bounded masculinity lessens, and the maturing man is freed from reliance on the bifurcated, phallicized manhood—typically requiring some sort of renunciation of what is relegated to the purportedly *feminine*—that was so adaptive earlier in life.

Here let me restate one of this book's key points: a *primary aim of analytic treatment is the resumption of unconscious bisexualization,* entailing ubiquitous and inescapable bigendered tensions. Masculine progression requires strengthening the capacity to hold and contain the inherent strain that emerges from the fluctuating prephallic, phallic, and genital positions, rather than dealing with such tensions primarily by resorting to foreclosing, evacuative, or idealizing defenses. The strengthened capacity to withstand these tensions results in a more flexible, fluid sense of maleness—a gender fluidity and bigenderality—that can access what is typically considered as inhabiting both masculine and feminine interiority.

In this final chapter, I will stress the role played by the analyst in facilitating the patient's progression to a maturing manhood. To reach the objective of helping our male patients attain a healthier, more mature sense of their maleness, I emphasize above all the importance of the analyst's capacity to achieve greater gender fluidity—and in particular, to arrive at what I describe as psychic *bigenderality*. For the male analyst, this often entails the capacity to incorporate and access what in more binary cultural thinking is regarded as feminine.

As a patient said to me at our last session, after we had worked together for nine years in intensive analytic therapy in which I inhabited male and female transference positions (and the patient spoke without consciously knowing of my own writings in the field):

> You've really been like a *father* to me ... a father surrogate, I suppose, and as a result, you've helped me find a *mother* inside! ... It's like now I have a kind of mother inside me that lets me just be with my feelings. Now I don't have to do something or try to get rid of those feelings, but rather just kind of hang with them.

Gender identity and the analyst: being "in" but not "of" the binary

Each analyst has his or her own unique notion of gender. Furthermore, because prejudices concerning gender identity issues inevitably exist in the minds of both patient and analyst, analysts need to interrogate and better understand both their patients' and their own conscious and unconscious gender identifications and prejudices (Cereijido 2019). As I highlight throughout this book, considerable tension remains at the heart of the attempt to grasp the nature of the masculine (and feminine). Freud himself conveyed caution as well as a sense of duality in thinking about psychosexuality, given the overlap yet disjunction between body and mind—specifically, in terms of how each individual must deal with the recognition of sexual difference.[1]

In thinking about the expanding boundaries of male gender identity and the theme of the feminine in males, many questions surface about womanhood and the way in which psychoanalytic and cultural prejudices—particularly overvalued traditional psychoanalytic ideas and beliefs—limit our understanding of patients and our own ideas about gender. As suggested in Chapter 1, it is crucial to recognize Freud's limitations when exploring the female's otherness from his perspective of masculine subjectivity—especially his view of the inexplicable and enigmatic, so-called *dark continent* of the feminine equated with the object of *lack* (originally, lack of the penis). Lacan (1949) reframed this "lack" as an inherent dimension of male and female self-representation as gendered—a "constitutive loss .... As psychic subjects we will never be whole" (Gulati and Pauley 2019, p. 103).

Freud's androcentric, phallic, binary view of the subject-object, masculine-feminine dualism, still rather rigidly held by some, is well explicated in Freud's (1918) argument as the basis for the male dread of women. He described the woman as "mysterious, strange and therefore apparently hostile," which causes the man to fear "being weakened by the woman, infected with her femininity and of then showing himself incapable" (p. 198).

I find myself imagining how psychoanalysis might have taken up these themes had Freud been born in 1956 rather than 1856, or even in 1986—and moreover, what if he had been born a female? Imagine, too, if Freud had access to the changes and understandings of the last half century, when credence is no longer easily given to the idea of an inescapable, biological or anatomical "destiny." Yet, despite providing neither a synthesis nor a resolution to the dilemma of sex and gender, Freud helped us see that psychosexuality rests on unconscious fantasies, meaning, and structures for which the body is the linchpin.

Today's theories and practices with regard to sexuality and gender are in widespread transition and, as I've mentioned, nuanced consideration of the concept of the masculine and feminine must include biologically sexed bodies, gender assignment at birth, multiple identifications, fields of desire and varied object choices, changing gender roles, and bisexual fantasies/bisexuality (Diamond 2020).[2] The complexity of venturing into this domain of bodily, subjective life that utilizes the lenses of gender as organizers is compounded by a lack of common definitions, as well as by frequent conflation of terms, and sizeable psychic tension accompanies the widely varied subjective ways of constructing one's sense of gender identity in the context of the masculine/feminine binary.

Despite the complexity of this venture, while risking inescapable and over-simplified reifications, I propose that although every female and male must *live in* this binary, in terms of the psyche, no one is *actually of* the binary. This sexual/gender binary, in its aim to provide order to internal and external life, inevitably "holds a grip on our thinking" (Scarfone 2019, p. 573); yet—as I've discussed in previous chapters—in terms of the largely unconscious psyche and the subjective position within, no one is actually *of* the binary. Moreover, it is useful to say again that, since sexed and gendered subjectivity is always organized in tension between the internal sense of gender identity and socio-cultural structures (Glocer Fiorini 2017), each of us faces unconscious struggles with highly charged and inherent conflicts around gender and sexuality.

This brings us back to the binary and whether there is a useful way to think of the feminine existing within the male interior beyond the binary realm. I believe that there is, and as I will elaborate in the next section, that the common stereotypical idea that women are more relationally oriented suggests a more complex form of a man's interiority signified by the term *inclusivity*. I will subsequently discuss how this pertains to the male analyst and the potentially transformative impact of the analytic relationship.

Bigenderality: psychic bisexuality and interiorized gender in the male analyst

It goes without saying that the analyst's gender is a significant factor in treatment, and that for the male analyst, the feminine offers particular challenges as well as opportunities to his sense of maleness. In general, these pertain to an *inclusivity and interiority* that can easily be foreclosed from a man's conscious experience. The highly unique experience of one's gender identity, in both conscious and unconscious forms, oscillates continually—and (as explored in my first three chapters) may do so even more in the male psyche, since the man's feminine identifications are particularly conflicted (Diamond 2006, 2009).

The center of the feminine, as discussed in Chapter 2, is constructed by unconscious archaic fantasies grounded in the female body (Balsam 2019). Overall, the uniqueness of internal space in the female body challenges both female and male analysts since the female genitalia create openings for unconscious invasion fantasies (Ellman 2019; Goodman 2019), as well as for the embracing of *otherness* within one's self. Regardless, the female genitalia, exciting and mysterious as they may be, are often disruptive for the male because they signify his primordial vulnerability—his own *dark hole*—occurring in his primary relationship to his mother's body (Diamond 2015).

As I will elaborate in aiming to help analysts more successfully bear the tensions related to the "feminine" otherness within, and in favoring the sophisticated thinking of contemporary feminist-oriented analysts, I contend that the feminine contained by the male analyst's psyche stands for the recognition and acknowledgment of the other within the self. It is vital for analysts to understand that while we live in a sexual (and gender) binary of male/female, we are not subjectively rooted within it; consequently, we remain capable of making use of feminine and masculine parts of ourselves—namely, by drawing on our inherent bigenderality wherein gender and sex are positioned in a less conflated way.

So how might we think more specifically about the "feminine" in the male analyst? There are at least four useful tropes in contemporary psychoanalytic thinking for re-imagining the feminine in both males and females (Diamond 2020). First, *receptivity* has surpassed passivity and lack (or absence) as the major trope (Fogel 1998; Mayer 1985), and the capacity for reverie is typically rendered as feminine or maternal. Second, *space* relates to the sense of the female genital and is contrasted with the "negative" feminine lack that long pervaded psychoanalytic phallocentric thinking (Bassin 1996; Elise 1997). Third, female *psychosexual desire* casts the double lips of the female mouth and genitals as representative of the "positive" feminine, which emerges from the very first erotic, labial strivings necessary to preserve the infant's life (Schiller 2012; see also Freud 1912). Simone de Beauvoir (1949) captured this in the sexual domain by suggesting that, when aroused, "while the man has a 'hard on,' the woman 'gets wet'" (p. 398). Parenthetically, we might note that wetness for men in the form of crying is often regarded as shameful. Finally, female *power*, along with potent generativity or *puissance* (Irigaray 1993), has been reconceived (contra "phallic power"), as emerging from a *matricial space* (Chetrit-Vatine 2014) that helps create bonds while reflecting the courage to accept vulnerability, limitation, and transience (Alizade 2009).

Similar to the masculine, the feminine within the psychoanalyst is not easily characterized and must withstand the ongoing problem of being conflated with *the* female and *the* maternal. Moreover, the very idea of the feminine in any male, let alone the male analyst, is fraught with difficulties, in part because its recognition requires disentangling femininity and masculinity from biological sex and easily overgeneralized notions of essentialism. In short, we must be cautious about implying any specific, normative metapsychological notions pertaining to gender, although, as alluded to earlier, I suggest that a useful realm for our discourse emerges from the common stereotype that women are more relationally oriented, which implies a more complex form of interiority signified by inclusiveness. I shall clarify this in what follows.

As noted, within our contemporary, Westernized frames of psychoanalytic thinking, interiority—the so-called dark continent of what remains largely unknown in the internal world—tends to be equated with the feminine. Moving beyond Freud's idea of passivity, such interiority tends to be signified by a more active receptivity that is understood as essential for the survival of both female and male infants. Nonetheless, equation of the feminine with receptivity is somewhat problematic for both genders; in males (and male analysts), receptivity fundamentally reinvokes the *primordial vulnerability* that is invariably accompanied by psychodynamic and sociocultural pressures to renounce such inherent receptivity—along with renouncing dependence on female caregivers and primary identifications with them. For many males, this can produce more rigid phallic defenses, misogyny, and *femiphobia*, which expresses the fretful repudiation of the feminine within (Diamond 2015). One of the main points stressed in this book is that such unyielding phallicity—as evident with Brad, the case discussed in Chapter 3—tends to defend against emasculation by evading the most threatening and most durable aspect of the male's psychic reality: namely, masculinity's containment of unsymbolizable, primordial vulnerability.

Because the mind/body is conceptualized as holding interiority, many analysts think of femininity as resting upon acknowledging "feelings about imaginings about *interior spaces*" (Goodman 2019, p. 89, italics added). From this perspective, procreative dreams, thoughts, and generative naming occur within feminine or female spaces.

It seems clear that there is no way to address the feminine in the male analyst (or in any male) without returning to Freud's (1905, 1925) sage insights about the human psyche's essential bisexuality. Yet, as noted earlier, I believe it may be more accurate to substitute the term *psychic bigenderality*, or *bigenderism*, of the human mind (Blechner 2015). These expressions can be further distinguished from the mind's sexuality, which in extending Freud's polymorphous perversity might more aptly be called *psychic ambisexuality*. Regardless of how certain any of us might be about being masculine or feminine (let alone a man or a woman), the sine qua non of psychoanalysis is that "the unconscious knows better" (Rose 2016, p. 8).

While there have been many efforts within the binary to explore the gendered facets of mental functioning, Winnicott (1971) offers especially useful clinical ideas in the context of object relating—ideas that extend the binary facet of Freudian thinking regarding fundamental psychic bisexuality. For instance, Winnicott posited the existence of "unalloyed male and female elements" in both males and females, to varying degrees (p. 79). The purely female element establishes the experience of *being*, whereas by contrast, the male element presupposes *separateness*. The male element *does* something—from which *finding* and *using* consequently arise—while the female element simply *is* and thus becomes the basis for the sense of *existing*.

In clinical analysis, it remains quite common to identify and describe "maternal" and "paternal" transferences, despite the recent blurring of lines between mothering and fathering as parental roles and the trend toward the de-gendering of parenting practices (Davies and Eagle 2013; Seidman and Frank 2019). Thus, psychoanalysts continue to find it useful to stipulate a dichotomous order of gendered representations in which the female element is largely operative in the maternal mode, while the male element tends to dominate in the paternal mode. It is crucial to recognize when employing binary terminology, however, that each individual carries a mixture of traits belonging to his or her own sex and to the opposite sex (Freud 1905). Moreover, given inherent psychic bigenderality, mothers and females (including female analysts) sometimes carry the paternal, and fathers and males (including male analysts) the maternal.

For the male or female analyst functioning with access to the feminine, the maternal mode of orientation toward the patient conveys a "soothing kind" of "joining" (McWilliams 1991, p. 525) that entails the function of taking in and holding *facets of the other inside one's self*—a state of mind that is extremely receptive to unconscious communication. This stance enables the analyst to experience nonverbal forms of communication, as well as unintegrated and disintegrated mental states (Diamond 1997, 2017b). This inherent analytic disposition, which may be given a gendered representation as a maternal womb, demands a "readiness to make oneself available to the analysand" (Scarfone 2019, p. 573). Such feminine receptivity is characterized by fluidity, space, containment, and being (Fogel 1998); consequently, the analyst listens in order to *hear meaning* (Parsons 2007) as it emerges primarily from his or her state of reverie.

Such maternal-like receptivity, in re-creating a dyadic, more fusional, mother-infant alliance, can enable the patient to experience unformulated, unintegrated, and even disintegrated dissociative states emerging out of trauma that allow for *being* and *becoming* (rather than knowledge and insight per se). Within this maternal order, the psychic functions of reception, gestation, delivery, and holding, as well as nonverbal forms of communication, are predominant (Bollas 2000). Also pertinent is the notion of *reverie*, in which a more passive and receptive orientation offering the space for something to develop is understood as an expression of the mother's love (Birksted-Breen 2016; Cegile 2013). In Bion's (1962, 1970) mother-infant terminology, the mother/therapist metabolizes her infant/patient's unprocessed beta elements through maternal reverie and alpha functioning, thereby providing the infant/patient with understanding and relief from unbearable anxieties.

So what does all this come down to for the male analyst at work?

The male analyst's "femininity" in the clinical context

In the context of object relating, the feminine in the male analyst basically reflects an embrace of the patient's otherness in a wider swath—which goes beyond the ideas of holding and containing—and instead stands for the analyst's recognition and acknowledgment of *the other within the self*. This emerges for the male analyst, then, as the female, the woman, the mother, the girl, and the baby within the analyst's self as these elements can come alive in his work with every patient, male or female. In this respect, the *interiority of the feminine* entails a subversion of the generally accepted gender dichotomy (Quindeau 2013), and the so-called feminine or maternal generative space—the other within the self—is recognized and protected, much as the mother's body supports and protects the fetus/baby *other* inside her (while ideally, the once-removed father or surrogate watchfully protects the mother-baby dyad).

This feminine, maternally generative, or "matricial" space of radical passivity—in terms of the analyst's ethical position—requires not acting when receiving from within one's own internal body (Chetrit-Vatine 2014).[3] Through inhabiting this feminine, matricial position, the analyst invites the patient's feelings and neediness that in turn can deluge the analytic space. Hence, in thinking within the culturally prevalent binary, the maternal/feminine order renders the individual, whether male or female, more capable of being receptive as well as invaded, of listening in an emotionally cathected way, recognizing alterity within both self and other, and consequently of both affirming and respecting the other's limits and strengths. Such "female fecundity" requires that we allow ourselves to be touched, penetrated, seduced, engulfed, deluged, and even taken hostage by the other's neediness, fragilities, and unrepresented or weakly represented psychic experiences (Balsam 2018).

In attempting to move outside the binary when discussing the male analyst, this is typically described as *gender fluidity, psychic bisexuality,* or *bigenderality*—the gender tertiary of a more universal fluidity—or even *transgenderality*. Arguably, within this interior and ambiguously gendered generative space, bisexual, same-sex, and cross-sex representations all find a place—as do varied fantasies and modes of achieving pleasure and escaping pain—and all these can border one another "without rejecting the unknown or the other in the sense of a clear dichotomous gender and/or sexual identity" (Quindeau 2013, p. 233). In fact, as discussed in Chapter 7, for a male patient's analysis to be considered successful, a genital organization must ultimately be established in which inside and outside—body, psyche, and external world—are linked in active relationship to one another (Balint 1950; see also Freud 1937). I wish to add that this is especially so for the male analysand undergoing a training analysis in order to become a competent psychoanalyst.

To the extent that this attainment is approximated in the clinical encounter, both time and space are necessary to allow for "digestion and transformation" (Birksted-Breen 2012, p. 833), which go well beyond reverie and make interpretation meaningful (Busch 2019). Like the mother during pregnancy, and perhaps like any human in relation to the other's alterity, *the feminine in the male analyst must carry the unformed or weakly represented until it is ready to be birthed or named*. This often entails allowing what is quite uncomfortable or unreachable to continue to exist while waiting until it is sufficiently formed and ready for delivery in an interpretive or reflective intervention.

In this respect, the male analyst is called upon to withdraw from his own phallic tendency to respond (i.e., what is often colloquially and more pejoratively referred to as *mansplaining*), and perhaps even from his primarily genital desires to connect to the other, and instead to live more easily with his own bigenderality. My work with Seth, the patient presented in Chapter 2, illustrates this through a generative form of waiting that required me to tolerate my own shame sufficiently to access my embodied reveries of being a small boy soothingly and playfully bathed and excited by my mother. The memory, which entailed transitory identifications as both a small child and a loving mother, helped open a more fluid, gendered space for me as Seth's analyst in order to receive an aspect of him that had remained unformed (*unbirthed*). This experience could then be utilized to move the analysis beyond an impasse, which enabled Seth to detoxify his own shame and more easily inhabit his own psychic bigenderality.

Overall summary and some concluding thoughts

In this book, I have discussed the theoretical roots of male gender identity, beginning with Freudian tenets and moving on through later psychoanalytic developments. Contemporary views on male gender identity—including and especially its consideration as a developmental trajectory with shifting balances among prephallic, phallic, and genital interior positions—have been presented; male gender identity is not seen as inborn and static, but rather as impacted by major influences. I have explored the shaping of masculinity in childhood, including the significance of actual and symbolic fathering, mothering, and the father-mother together. I have noted the three-part nature of father functioning, encompassing attracting, separating, and watchfully protective features. Social, cultural, and biological influences on masculinity and gender have been considered, and the concept of the male ego ideal has been discussed in depth. In midlife and later life, a more rigid idea of masculinity is more likely to give way to gender fluidity, as I have described in some detail. Finally, I have explored themes of gender, bigenderality, and masculinity/femininity as pervasive factors in psychoanalytic practice.

In the end, the fully becoming man who has attained access to both the gendered and nongendered multitude within has largely transcended the need for a clearly defined, well-bounded masculine gender identity. As discussed in Chapter 5, his masculine identity will have been largely built on his mother's unconscious attitudes toward his maleness; furthermore, from the onset of life, the male infant's *primordial vulnerability* includes the *proto-genital masculine essence,* as discussed in Chapter 7—that is, "typically feminine" qualities that stand in opposition to the penetrating, more boundaried and exterior ones associated with phallicism.

The maturing man, in consolidating his masculinity, is freed from his reliance on the bifurcated, phallicized gender identity of manhood that played an important and frequently beneficial role in his childhood, youthful, and younger-adult adaptations. The challenge for the aging man necessitates coming to terms with parts of his psyche that were necessarily renounced or repudiated earlier in order to establish a stable sense of identity. Indeed, as emphasized in the previous two chapters, the *sense of masculinity always involves loss, lack, and lifelong conflicts, tensions, and challenges* pertaining to gendered *ego ideals.* Furthermore, to reiterate, *masculinity always remains tenuous,* despite the maturing man's ability to contain and even embrace the strain of its conflictual nature and irreducible predicament.

In striving to achieve the genital ego ideal, a man gains access to receptivity and other so-called typically feminine traits residing deep within the male interior. This more mature form of manhood, signified by a more flexible, fluid sense of gender identity ideally attained at midlife, represents a movement away from a man's experience of being at the center of his odyssey—as epitomized by the mythic Odysseus, whose journeys take him far from his Penelope and Telemachus—and perhaps to a more Zeus-like form in which, as happened for the mature Odysseus returning to Ithaca, his watchfulness can protect his progeny. For some men, it is only in older age that the object dependence of human existence, "the first fact of life," is no longer denied; finally, the illusory Western attitude of autonomous individuality can be overcome and our fundamentally relational nature is fully embraced (Teising 2008).

The transformed, less gendered—or perhaps more aptly considered *multigendered* or *bigendered*—ego ideal can be heard in Walt Whitman's (1855) timeless ode to the fluid interiority of a more fully realized manhood:

> I am of old and young, of the foolish as much as the wise,
> Regardless of others, ever regardful of others,
> Maternal as well as paternal, a child as well as a man.
>
> [*Leaves of Grass*, 16:326–328]

While I have offered my thoughts on a healthier, broadened sense of maleness that incorporates what I term *psychic bigenderality* as well as greater gender fluidity, we must recognize that, as noted, masculinity remains conflictual and inherently elusive; it is located at the junction of unconscious psychodynamics and familial, cultural, and biological influences. When we consider masculinity at this crossroads, dichotomous, binary terminology tends to conflate the interior and exterior realms. For the male in particular, a helpless dependency on the mother creates a *primordial vulnerability* that remains at the core of the self as an enduring sense of deficit, lack, and insufficiency—an essential sense of shortcoming that subsequent defenses and ego ideals can partially modulate, yet never fully resolve. Consequently, masculinity requires affirmation (or its reaction formation) and persists as an irreducible predicament that, as Donald Moss (2012) lucidly reminds us, "enduringly resist[s] capture by reason" (p. 6). Masculinity perseveres in its somewhat fragile visage, as discussed at length in earlier chapters; it does not simply progress in a linear way, nor does it necessarily manifest normativity or steadiness.

In closing, then, I find myself continuing to ponder the highly charged, ever-present, and inherent conflicts around gender and sexuality as I ask myself: How much of my life as a heterosexual man has required great care in revealing—or, perhaps more accurately, in navigating or even disguising—what might not be so easily acceptable in the phallocentric, binary world of gendered appearances? Indeed, despite our achievement of a degree of gender fluidity as it reflects maturing manhood—which I deem especially necessary for psychoanalysts—perhaps we are all destined to fail in individually unique ways in our quest to perform gender. Ideally, however, this quest results in a degree of invaluable, transformative insight—perhaps fostered by the psychoanalytic experience—that would not otherwise have been attained.

Notes

1 It has been argued that the Freudian disjunction between biology and psychology is greatest in relation to women, wherein the very attempt to comprehend the nature of femininity cannot be grasped yet must be tolerated; hence, it becomes increasingly "out of focus" (Birksted-Breen 1993, p. 4).
2 *Bisexuality* remains an overly saturated, ambiguous term encompassing cross-gender identifications, roles, and object choices, though colloquially it pertains strictly to sexual object choice (Blechner 2015).
3 This is closely related to Gitelson's (1962) use of Spitz's (1956) concept of the *diatrophic function,* wherein the analyst's healing intention comes alive through an affirmative (albeit regressive) countertransference emerging in the form of erupting instincts to revive and support the patient's developmental drive.

References

Abelin, E. L. (1971). The role of the father in the separation-individuation process. In *Separation-Individuation*, ed. J. B. McDevitt & C. F. Settlage. New York: International Universities Press, pp. 229–252.

Abelin, E. L. (1975). Some further observations and comments on the earliest role of the father. *Int. J. Psychoanal.*, 56:293–302.

Abelin, E. L. (1980). Triangulation, the role of the father and the origins of core gender identity during the rapprochement subphase. In *Rapprochement: The Critical Subphase of Separation-Individuation*, ed. R. F. Lax, S. Bach & J. A. Burland. New York: Aronson, pp. 151–169.

Aisenstein, M. (2015). The question of the father in 2015. *Psychoanal. Q.*, 84:351–362.

Alizade, M. (2009). Femininity and the human dimension. In *On Freud's "Femininity,"* ed. L. Glocer Fiorini & G. Abelin-Sas. London: Karnac, pp. 198–211.

Aron, L. (1995). The internalized primal scene. *Psychoanal. Dialogues*, 5:195–237.

Auchincloss, E. L. & Michels, R. (1989). The impact of middle age on ambitions and ideals. In *The Middle Years: New Psychoanalytic Perspectives*, ed. J. M. Oldham & R. S. Liebert. New Haven, CT: Yale University Press, pp. 40–57.

Axelrod, S. D. (1995). Men and work: aspects of a deep structure of masculinity. Paper presented at the Spring Meeting of the Division of Psychoanalysis (39) of the American Psychological Association, Santa Monica, CA, April.

Axelrod, S. D. (1997). Developmental pathways to masculinity: a reconsideration of Greenson's "disidentifying from mother." *Issues Psychoanal. Psychol.*, 19:101–115.

Balint, M. (1948). On genital love. *Int. J. Psychoanal.*, 29:34–40.

Balint, M. (1950). On the termination of analysis. *Int. J. Psychoanal.*, 31:196–199.

Balsam, R. (2001). Integrating male and female elements in a woman's gender identity. *J. Amer. Psychoanal. Assn.*, 49:1335–1360.

Balsam, R. (2018). Response to John Steiner's "overcoming obstacles in analysis: is it possible to relinquish omnipotence and accept receptive femininity?" *Psychoanal. Q.*, 87:21–31.

Balsam, R. (2019). From the "child woman" to "wonder woman": progress and misogyny in psychoanalytic theory and clinical work. In *Changing Notions of the Feminine: Confronting Psychoanalysts' Prejudices*, ed. M. Cereijido. London: Routledge, pp. 12–31.

Baron-Cohen, S. (2003). *The Essential Difference: The Truth about the Male and Female Brain*. New York: Basic Books.

Baron-Cohen, S. (2007). The evolution of empathizing and systemizing: assortative mating of two strong systemizers and the cause of autism. In *The Oxford Handbook of Evolutionary Psychology*, ed. L. Barrett & R. Dunbar. Oxford, UK: Oxford University Press.

Baron-Cohen, S., Lutchmaya, S. & Knickmeyer, R. (2005). *Prenatal Testosterone in Mind: Amniotic Fluid Studies*. Boston, MA: MIT Press/Bradford Books.

Barratt, B. B. (2019). Oedipality and oedipal complexes reconsidered: on the incest taboo as key to the universality of the human condition. *Int. J. Psychoanal.*, 100:7–31.

Bassin, D. (1996). Beyond the he and she: toward the reconciliation of masculinity and femininity in the postoedipal female mind. *J. Amer. Psychoanal. Assn.*, 44(suppl.):157–190.

de Beauvoir, S. (1949). *The Second Sex*, trans. C. Borde & S. Malovany-Chevallier. New York: Vintage Books, 2011.

Behrends, R. S. & Blatt, S. J. (1985). Internalized psychological development throughout the life cycle. *Psychoanal. Study Child*, 40:11–39.

Benedek, T. (1970). Fatherhood and providing. In *Parenthood*, ed. E. J. Anthony & T. Benedek. Boston: Little, Brown, pp. 167–183.

Benjamin, J. (1988). *The Bonds of Love*. New York: Pantheon Books.

Benjamin, J. (1991). Father and daughter: identification with a difference—a contribution to gender heterodoxy. *Psychoanal. Dialogues*, 1:277–299.

Benjamin, J. (1996). In defense of gender ambiguity. *Gender & Psychoanal.*, 1:27–43.

Bertrand, M. & Pan, J. (2013). The trouble with boys: social influences and the gender gap in disruptive behavior. *Amer. Econ. J. Appl. Econ.*, 5:32–64.

Betcher, W. & Pollack, W. (1993). *In a Time of Fallen Heroes: The Re-Creation of Masculinity*. New York: Atheneum.

Bion, W. R. (1959). Attacks on linking. *Int. J. Psychoanal.*, 40:308–315.

Bion, W. R. (1961). *Experiences in Groups and Other Papers*. New York: Basic Books.

Bion, W. R. (1962). The psycho-analytic theory of thinking. *Int. J. Psychoanal.*, 43:444–469.

Bion, W. R. (1965). *Transformations: Change from Learning to Growth*. London: Tavistock.

Bion, W. R., ed. (1970). Container and contained. In *Attention and Interpretation*. London: Karnac, pp. 72–82.

Birksted-Breen, D. (1993). Introduction. In *The Gender Conundrum: Contemporary Psychoanalytic Perspectives on Femininity and Masculinity*, ed. D. Birksted-Breen. London: Routledge, pp. 1–39.

Birksted-Breen, D. (1996). Phallus, penis and mental space. *Int. J. Psychoanal.*, 77:649–657.

Birksted-Breen, D. (2012). Taking time: the tempo of psychoanalysis. *Int. J. Psychoanal.*, 93:819–835.

Birksted-Breen, D. (2016). Bi-ocularity, the functioning mind of the psychoanalyst. *Int. J. Psychoanal.*, 97:25–40.

Blake, W. (1789). *Songs of Innocence and of Experience: Shewing the Two Contrary States of the Human Soul, 1789-1794*. Oxford, UK: Oxford University Press.

Blanck-Cereijido, F. (2019). Motherhood and new reproductive technologies: an overview of the last twenty-five years. In *Changing Notions of the Feminine: Confronting Psychoanalysts' Prejudices*, ed. M. Cereijido. London: Routledge, pp. 68–74.

Blechner, M. (2015). Bigenderism and bisexuality. *Contemp. Psychoanal.*, 51: 503–522.

Blos, P. (1984). Son and father. *J. Amer. Psychoanal. Assn.*, 32:301–324.

Blos, P. (1985). *Son and Father: Before and Beyond the Oedipus Complex*. New York: Free Press.

Boehm, F. (1930). The femininity complex in men. *Int. J. Psychoanal.*, 11:444–469.

Bollas, C. (2000). *Hysteria*. New York: Routledge.

Bollas, C. (2011). *The Christopher Bollas Reader*. New York: Routledge.

Bowlby, J. (1988). *A Secure Base: Parent-Child Attachment and Healthy Human Development*. New York: Basic Books.

Braunschweig, D. & Fain, M. (1978). The phallic shadow. In *The Gender Conundrum*, ed. D. Breen. London: Routledge, 1993, pp. 130–144.

Britton, R. (1989). The missing link: parental sexuality in the Oedipus complex. In *The Oedipus Complex Today*, ed. J. Steiner. London: Karnac, pp. 83–102.

Bromberg, P. (1998). *Standing in the Spaces: Essays on Clinical Process, Trauma, and Dissociation*. Hillsdale, NJ: Analytic Press.

Busch, F. (2019). *The Analyst's Reveries: Explorations in Bion's Enigmatic Concept*. London: Routledge.

Butler, J. (1995). Melancholy gender-refused identification. *Psychoanal. Dialogues*, 5:165–180.

Caper, R. (2017). Containment, self-containment and psychological growth: a contribution to Wilfred Bion's theory of the container. Paper presented at 50th Congress of International Psychoanalytical Association, Buenos Aires, Argentina.

Cath, S. H., Gurwitt, A. & Gunsberg, L., eds. (1989). *Fathers and Their Families*. Hillsdale, NJ: Analytic Press.

Cath, S. H., Gurwitt, A. & Ross, J. M., eds. (1982). *Father and Child: Developmental and Clinical Perspectives*. Boston, MA: Little, Brown & Co.

Cegile, G. R. D. (2013). Orientation, containment, and the emergence of symbolic thinking. *Int. J. Psychoanal.*, 94:1077–1091.

Celenza, A. (2010). Similarities with a (crucial) difference: reply to commentaries by Shapiro and Marshall. *Stud. Gender Sex.*, 11:200–204.

Cereijido, M., ed. (2019). *Changing Notions of the Feminine: Confronting Psychoanalysts' Prejudices*. London/New York: Routledge.

Chasseguet-Smirgel, J., ed. (1964). Feminine guilt and the Oedipus complex. In *Female Sexuality*. London: Karnac, 1985, pp. 94–134.

Chasseguet-Smirgel, J. (1976). Freud and female sexuality: the consideration of some blind spots in the exploration of the "Dark Continent." *Int. J. Psychoanal.*, 57:275–286.

Chasseguet-Smirgel, J. (1984). *Creativity and Perversion*. New York: Norton.

Chasseguet-Smirgel, J. (1985). *The Ego Ideal*. New York: Norton.

Chetrit-Vatine, V. (2014). *The Ethical Seduction of the Analytic Situation: The Feminine-Maternal Origins of Responsibility for the Other*. London: Karnac.

Chodorow, N. J. (1978). *The Reproduction of Mothering*. Berkeley, CA: University of California Press.

Chodorow, N. J. (1994). *Femininities, Masculinities, Sexualities: Freud and Beyond.* Lexington, KY: University Press of Kentucky.

Chodorow, N. J. (1996). Theoretical gender and clinical gender. *J. Amer. Psychoanal. Assn.*, 44(suppl.):215–238.

Chodorow, N. J. (2004). The American independent tradition: Loewald, Erikson, and the (possible) rise of intersubjective ego psychology. *Psychoanal. Dialogues*, 14:207–232.

Chodorow, N. J. (2012). *Individualizing Gender and Sexuality: Theory and Practice.* New York: Routledge.

Christiansen, A. (1996). Masculinity and its vicissitudes: reflections on some gaps in the psychoanalytic theory of male identity formation. *Psychoanal. Rev.*, 83:97–124.

Civitarese, G. (2013). *The Violence of Emotions: Bion and Post-Bionian Psychoanalysis.* London: Routledge.

Colarusso, C. A. (1997). Separation-individuation processes in middle adulthood: the fourth individuation. In *The Seasons of Life: Separation-Individuation Perspectives*, ed. S. Akhtar & S. Kramer. Northvale, NJ: Aronson, pp. 73–94.

Colarusso, C. A. (2000). Separation-individuation phenomena in adulthood. *J. Amer. Psychoanal. Assn.*, 48:1467–1489.

Corbett, K. (2001). More life: centrality and marginality in human development. *Psychoanal. Dialogues*, 11:313–335.

Corbett, K. (2003). Pride/power/penis. Paper presented at the Spring Meeting of the Division of Psychoanalysis (39) of the American Psychological Association, Minneapolis, MN, April.

Corbett, K. (2009). *Boyhoods: Rethinking Masculinities.* New Haven, CT: Yale University Press.

Corbett, K. (2011). Gender regulation. *Psychoanal. Q.*, 80:441–459.

Cortes, L. R., Cistemas, C. D. & Forger, N. G. (2019). Does gender leave an epigenetic impact on the brain? *Front Neurosci.*, 13:1–7.

Cournut, J. (1998). Poor men—or why men are afraid of women. In *Reading French Psychoanalysis*, ed. D. Birksted-Breen, S. Flanders & A. Gibeault. London: Routledge, 2010, pp. 601–622.

David, C. (1973). The beautiful differences. In *Reading French Psychoanalysis*, ed. D. Birksted-Breen, S. Flanders & A. Gibeault. London: Routledge, 2010, pp. 649–667.

Davies, N. & Eagle, G. (2013). Conceptualizing the paternal function: maleness, masculinity, or thirdness? *Contemp. Psychoanal.*, 49:559–585.

Diamond, M. J. (1986). Becoming a father: a psychoanalytic perspective on the forgotten parent. *Psychoanal. Rev.*, 73:445–468.

Diamond, M. J. (1995). Someone to watch over me: the father as the original protector of the mother-infant dyad. *Psychoanal. Psychother.*, 12:89–102.

Diamond, M. J. (1997). Boys to men: the maturing of masculine gender identity through paternal watchful protectiveness. *Gender & Psychoanal.*, 2:443–468.

Diamond, M. J. (1998). Fathers with sons: psychoanalytic perspectives on "good enough" fathering throughout the life cycle. *Gender & Psychoanal.*, 3:243–299.

Diamond, M. J. (2004a). Accessing the multitude within: a psychoanalytic perspective on the transformation of masculinity at mid-life. *Int. J. Psychoanal.*, 85:45–64.

Diamond, M. J. (2004b). The shaping of masculinity: revisioning boys turning away from their mothers to construct male gender identity. *Int. J. Psychoanal.*, 85:359–380.

Diamond, M. J. (2006). Masculinity unraveled: the roots of male gender identity and the shifting of male ego ideals throughout life. *J. Amer. Psychoanal. Assn.*, 54:1099–1130.

Diamond, M. J. (2007). *My Father Before Me: How Fathers and Sons Influence Each Other Throughout Their Lives*. New York: Norton.

Diamond, M. J. (2009). Masculinity and its discontents: making room for the "mother" inside the male—an essential achievement for healthy male gender identity. In *Heterosexual Masculinities*, ed. B. Reis & R. Grossmark. New York: Routledge, pp. 23–53.

Diamond, M. J. (2014). Analytic mind use and interpsychic communication: driving force in analytic technique, pathway to unconscious mental life. *Psychoanal. Q.*, 83:525–563.

Diamond, M. J. (2015). The elusiveness of masculinity: primordial vulnerability, lack, and the challenges of male development. *Psychoanal. Q.*, 84:47–102.

Diamond, M. J. (2017a). Recovering the father in mind and flesh: history, triadic functioning, and developmental implications. *Psychoanal. Q.*, 86:297–334.

Diamond, M. J. (2017b). The missing father function in psychoanalytic theory and technique: the analyst's internal couple and maturing intimacy. *Psychoanal. Q.*, 86:861–887.

Diamond, M. J. (2018). When fathering fails: violence, narcissism, and the father function in ancient tales and clinical analysis. *J. Amer. Psychanal. Assn.*, 66:7–40.

Diamond, M. J. (2020). The elusiveness of "the feminine" in the male analyst: *living in* yet not *being of* the binary. *Psychoanal. Q.*, 89:503–526.

Dio Bleichmar, E. (1995). The secret in the constitution of female sexuality: the effects of the adult's sexual look upon the subjectivity of the girl. *J. Clin. Psychoanal.*, 4:331–342.

Drury, S. S., Theall, K., Gleason, M. M., Smyke, A. T., De Vivo, I., Wong, J. Y. Y., Fox, N. A., Zeanah, C. H. & Nelson, C. A. (2012). Telomere length and early severe social deprivation: linking early adversity and cellular aging. *Mol. Psychiatry*, 17:719–772.

Ducat, S. J. (2004). *The Wimp Factor: Gender Gaps, Holy Wars, and the Politics of Anxious Masculinity*. Boston, MA: Beacon Press.

Dunn, S, ed. (2004). Achilles in love. In *The Insistence of Beauty*. New York: Norton, pp. 66–67.

Edgcumbe, R. & Burgner, M. (1975). The phallic-narcissistic phase: a differentiation between preoedipal and oedipal aspects of phallic development. *Psychoanal. Study Child*, 30:161–180.

Ehrensaft, D. (1987). *Parenting Together*. New York: Free Press.

Eizirik, C. L. (2015). The father, the father function, and the father principle: some contemporary psychoanalytic developments. *Psychoanal. Q.*, 84: 335–350.

Elise, D. (1996). Gender repertoire: body, mind and bisexuality. Paper presented at the Spring Meeting of the Division of Psychoanalysis (39) of the American Psychological Association, New York, April.

Elise, D. (1997). Primary femininity, bisexuality, and the female ego ideal: a reexamination of female developmental theory. *Psychoanal. Q.*, 66:489–517.

Elise, D. (1998). Gender repertoire: body, mind and bisexuality. *Psychoanal. Dialogues*, 8:353–371.

Elise, D. (2001). Unlawful entry: male fears of psychic penetration. *Psychoanal. Dialogues*, 11:499–531.

Ellman, P. L. (2019). When pain takes hold of the dyad: trauma and compromise in the female psyche. In *Changing Notions of the Feminine: Confronting Psychoanalysts' Prejudices*, ed. M. Cereijido. London: Routledge, pp. 44–56.

Erikson, E. H. (1950). *Childhood and Society*. New York: Norton, 1963.

Faimberg, H. (2004). *The Telescoping of Generations*. London: Karnac.

Fast, I. (1984). *Gender Identity*. Hillsdale, NJ: Analytic Press.

Fast, I. (1990). Aspects of early gender development: toward a reformulation. *Psychoanal. Psychol.*, 7(suppl.):105–117.

Fast, I. (1994). Women's capacity to give birth: a sex-difference issue for men? *Psychoanal. Dialogues*, 4:51–68.

Fast, I. (1995). Freud's theory of gender development of boys: some problems. Paper presented at the Spring Meeting of the Division of Psychoanalysis (39) of the American Psychological Association, Santa Monica, CA, April.

Fast, I. (1999). Aspects of core gender identity. *Psychoanal. Dialogues*, 9:633–661.

Fast, I. (2001). Boys will be boys! A contested aspect of gender development. Paper presented at the Spring Meeting of the Division of Psychoanalysis (39) of the American Psychological Association, Santa Fe, NM, April.

Fearon, R. P., Bakermans-Kranenburg, M. J., Van Ijzendoorn, M. H., Lapsley, A. & Roisman, G. I. (2010). The significance of insecure attachment and disorganization in the development of children's externalizing behavior: a meta-analytic study. *Child Dev.*, 81:435–456.

Figlio, K. (2010). Phallic and seminal masculinity: a theoretical and clinical confusion. *Int. J. Psychoanal.*, 91:119–139.

Fivaz-Depeursinge, E. & Corboz-Warnevy, A. (1999). *The Primary Triangle: A Developmental Systems View of Mothers, Fathers, and Infants*. New York: Basic Books.

Fivaz-Depeursinge, E., Lavanchy-Scaiola, C. & Favez, N. (2010). The young infant's triangular communication in the family: access to threesome intersubjectivity? Conceptual considerations and case illustrations. *Psychoanal. Dialogues*, 20:125–140.

Fogel, G. L. (1998). Interiority and inner genital space in men: what else can be lost in castration. *Psychoanal. Q.*, 67:662–697.

Fogel, G. L. (2006). Riddles of masculinity: gender, bisexuality, and thirdness. *J. Amer. Psychoanal. Assn.*, 54:1139–1163.

Fonagy, P. (2001). *Attachment Theory and Psychoanalysis*. New York: Other Press.

Fonagy, P. & Target, M. (1996). Playing with reality: I, theory of mind and the normal development of psychic reality. *Int. J. Psychoanal.*, 77:217–233.

Fraiberg, S., Edelson, E. & Shapiro, V. (1975). Ghosts in the nursery: a psychoanalytic approach to the problems of impaired infant-mother relationships. *J. Amer. Acad. Child Adolesc. Psychiatry*, 14:387–421.

Freud, S. (1895). Project for a scientific psychology. *S. E.*, 1:175.

Freud, S. (1900). The interpretation of dreams. *S. E.*, 4/5.

Freud, S. (1905). Three essays on the theory of sexuality. *S. E.*, 7:130–243.

Freud, S. (1907). The sexual enlightenment of children. *S. E.*, 9:129–139.

Freud, S. (1910). A special type of choice of object made by men (contributions to the psychology of love I). *S. E.*, 11:163–175.

Freud, S. (1912). On the universal tendency to debasement in the sphere of love. *S. E.*, 11:179–190.

Freud, S. (1913). Totem and taboo: some points of agreement between the mental lives of savages and neurotics. *S. E.*, 13:1–161.

Freud, S. (1918). From the history of an infantile neurosis (the "Wolf-Man"). *S. E.*, 17:1–122.

Freud, S. (1921). Group psychology and the analysis of the ego. *S. E.*, 18:65–143.

Freud, S. (1923). The infantile genital organization: an interpolation into the theory of sexuality. *S. E.*, 19:139–145.

Freud, S. (1924). The dissolution of the Oedipus complex. *S. E.*, 19:171–179.

Freud, S. (1925). Some psychical consequences of the anatomical distinction between the sexes. *S. E.*, 19:243–258.

Freud, S. (1930). Civilization and its discontents. *S. E.*, 21:59–145.

Freud, S. (1937). Analysis terminable and interminable. *S. E.*, 23:211–253.

Freud, S. (1939). Moses and monotheism. *S. E.*, 23:3–140.

Friedman, R. (1996). The role of the testicles in male psychological development. *J. Amer. Psychoanal. Assn.*, 44:201–253.

Friedman, R. C. & Downey, J. L. (2008). Sexual differentiation of behavior: the foundation of a developmental model of psychosexuality. *J. Amer. Psychoanal. Assn.*, 56:147–175.

Frommer, M. S. (1994). Homosexuality and psychoanalysis: technical considerations revisited. *Psychoanal. Dialogues*, 4:215–233.

Frommer, M. S. (2000). Offending gender: being and wanting in male same-sex desire. *Stud. Gender Sex.*, 1:191–206.

Gershwin, G. & Gershwin, I. (1926). Someone to Watch Over Me (from *Oh, Kay*). New York: Warner Bros. Music Corp.

Gherovici, P. (2019). Commentary on Gulati and Pauley. *J. Amer. Psychoanal. Assn.*, 67:123–132.

Gilmore, D. D. (1990). *Manhood in the Making*. New Haven, CT: Yale University Press.

Gitelson, M. (1962). The curative factors in psycho-analysis. *Int. J. Psychoanal.*, 43:194–205.

Glasser, M. (1985). The "weak spot"—some observations on male sexuality. *Int. J. Psychoanal.*, 66:405–414.

Glocer Fiorini, L. (2007). *Deconstructing the Feminine: Psychoanalysis, Gender, and Theories of Complexity*. London: Karnac.

Glocer Fiorini, L, ed. (2013). Deconstructing the paternal function—paternal function or third-party function? In *Sexual Difference in Debate: Bodies, Desires, and Fictions*. London: Karnac.

Glocer Fiorini, L, ed. (2017). *Sexual Difference in Debate: Bodies, Desires, and Fictions*. London: Karnac.

Glocer Fiorini, L. (2019). Deconstructing the feminine: discourses, logics and power. Theoretico-clinical implications. *Int. J. Psychoanal.*, 100:593–603.

Goldner, V. (2002). Toward a critical relational theory of gender. In *Gender and Psychoanalytic Space: Between Clinic and Culture*, ed. M. Dimen & V. Goldner. New York: Other Press, pp. 63–90.

Gonzalez, F. J. (2013). Another eden: proto-gay desire and social precocity. *Stud. Gender Sex.*, 13:112–121.

Goodman, N. R. (2019). Femininity: transforming prejudices in society and in psychoanalytic thought. In *Changing Notions of the Feminine: Confronting Psychoanalysts' Prejudices*, ed. M. Cereijido. London: Routledge, pp. 83–94.

Green, A, ed. (1986). The dead mother. In *On Private Madness*. New York: International Universities Press, pp. 142–173.

Green, A. (2004). Thirdness and psychoanalytic concepts. *Psychoanal. Q.*, 73:99–135.

Green, A. (2009). The construction of the lost father. In *The Dead Father: A Psychoanalytic Inquiry*, ed. L. Kalinich & S. Taylor. London: Routledge, pp. 23–46.

Greenberg, M. & Morris, N. (1974). Engrossment: the newborn's impact upon the father. *Amer. J. Orthopsychiatry*, 44:520–531.

Greenson, R. R. (1968). Disidentifying from mother—its special importance for the boy. *Int. J. Psychoanal.*, 49:370–374.

Greenspan, S. I. (1982). "The second other": the role of the father in early personality formation and the dyadic-phallic phase of development. In *Father and Child: Developmental and Clinical Perspectives*, ed. S. H. Cath, A. R. Gurwitt & J. M. Ross. Boston, MA: Little, Brown & Co., pp. 123–138.

Grunberger, B. (1964). Über das phallische. *Psyche—Z Psychoanal.*, 17:604–620.

Gulati, R. & Pauley, D. (2019). The half embrace of psychic bisexuality. *J. Amer. Psychoanal. Assn.*, 67:97–121.

Gurwitt, A. R. (1976). Aspects of prospective fatherhood: a case report. *Psychoanal. Study Child*, 31:237–271.

Gutmann, D. L. (1964). An exploration of ego configurations in middle and later life. In *Personality and Later Life*, ed. B. L. Neugarten. New York: Atherton, pp. 114–148.

Hansell, J. H. (1998). Gender anxiety, gender melancholia, gender perversion. *Psychoanal. Dialogues*, 8:337–351.

Hansell, J. H. (2011). Where sex was, there shall gender be? The dialectics of psychoanalytic gender theory. *Psychoanal. Q.*, 80:55–71.

Harris, A. (1991). Gender as contradiction. *Psychoanal. Dialogues*, 1:197–224.

Harris, A. (2005). Gender in linear and nonlinear history. *J. Amer. Psychoanal. Assn.*, 53:1079–1095.

Harris, A. (2008). Fathers and daughters. *Psychoanal. Inquiry*, 28:39–59.

Heenen-Wolff, S. (2011). Infantile bisexuality and the "complete oedipal complex": Freudian views on heterosexuality and homosexuality. *Int. J. Psychoanal.*, 92:1209–1220.

Herzog, J. M. (1982a). On father hunger: the father's role in the modulation of aggressive drive and fantasy. In *Father and Child*, ed. S. H. Cath, A. R. Gurwitt & J. M. Ross. Boston, MA: Little, Brown, pp. 163–174.

Herzog, J. M. (1982b). Patterns of expectant fatherhood: a study of the fathers of a group of premature infants. In *Father and Child*, ed. S. H. Cath, A. R. Gurwitt & J. M. Ross. Boston, MA: Little, Brown, pp. 301–314.

Herzog, J. M. (2001). *Father Hunger*. Hillsdale, NJ: Analytic Press.

Herzog, J. M. (2004). Father hunger and narcissistic deformation. *Psychoanal. Q.*, 73:893–914.

Herzog, J. M. (2005a). Triadic reality and the capacity to love. *Psychoanal. Q.*, 74:1029–1052.

Herzog, J. M. (2005b). What fathers do and how they do it. In *What Do Mothers Want?* ed. S. F. Brown. Hillsdale, NJ: Analytic Press, pp. 55–68.

Herzog, J. M. (2009). Constructing and deconstructing the conglomerate: thoughts about the father in life, in death, and in theory. In *The Dead Father: A Psychoanalytic Inquiry*, ed. L. Kalinich & S. Taylor. London: Routledge, pp. 133–143.

Horney, K. (1932). Observation on a specific difference in the dread felt by men and by women respectively for the opposite sex. *Int. J. Psychoanal.*, 13:348–360.

Horney, K. (1933). The denial of the vagina—a contribution to the problem of the genital anxieties specific to women. *Int. J. Psychoanal.*, 14:57–70.

Irigaray, L. (1993). *An Ethics of Sexual Difference*, trans. C. Porter. Ithaca, NY: Cornell University Press.

Isay, R. A. (1989). *Being Homosexual*. New York: Farrar, Strauss & Giroux.

Jacques, E. (1965). Death and the mid-life crisis. *Int. J. Psychoanal.*, 46:502–514.

Jay, M. (2007). Melancholy femininity and obsessive-compulsive masculinity: sex differences in melancholy gender. *Stud. Gender Sex.*, 8:115–135.

Jones, E. (1933). The phallic phase. *Int. J. Psychoanal.*, 14:1–33.

Jones, E. (1935). Early female sexuality. *Int. J. Psychoanal.*, 16:263–273.

Jung, C. G. (1934). The development of personality. In *Collected Works, Vol. 17*. Princeton, NJ: Princeton University Press, pp. 167–186.

Kaftal, E. (1991). On intimacy between men. *Psychoanal. Dialogues*, 1:305–328.

Kestenberg, J. (1968). Outside and inside: male and female. *J. Amer. Psychoanal. Assn.*, 16:457–520.

Klein, M. ed. (1928). Early stages of the Oedipus conflict. In *Love, Guilt and Reparation and Other Works, 1921–1945*. London: Hogarth Press, pp. 186–198.

Klein, M. (1932). *The Psychoanalysis of Children*, trans. A. Strachey. London: Hogarth Press.

Klein, M, ed. (1935). A contribution to the psychogenesis of manic-depressive states. In *Love, Guilt, and Reparation: The Writings of Melanie Klein, Vol. I*. London: Hogarth Press, pp. 236–289.

Kochanska, G., Coy, K. C. & Murray, K. T. (2001). The development of self-regulation in the first four years of life. *Child Dev.*, 72:1091–1111.

Kohut, H. (1971). *The Analysis of the Self*. New York: International Universities Press.

Kristeva, J. (2014). Reliance, or maternal eroticism. *J. Amer. Psychoanal. Assn.*, 62:69–85.

Kristeva, J. (2019). Prelude to an ethics of the feminine. Paper presented at 51st Congress of the International Psychoanalytical Association, London, England.

Kulish, N. (2000). Primary femininity: clinical advances and theoretical ambiguities. *J. Amer. Psychoanal. Assn.*, 48:1355–1379.

Labouvie-Vief, G. (1994). *Psyche and Eros: Mind and Gender in the Life Course*. Cambridge, UK: Cambridge University. Press.

Lacan, J. (1949). The mirror stage as formative of the *I* function as revealed in psychoanalytic experience. In *Écrits: The First Complete Edition in English*, trans. B. Fink. New York: Norton, 2006, pp. 75–81.

Lacan, J. (1953). The function and field of speech and language in psychoanalysis. In *Écrits: The First Complete Edition in English*, trans. B. Fink. New York: Norton, 2006, pp. 197–268.

Lacan, J. (1962). *The Seminar of Jacques Lacan, Book X, Anxiety*, trans. C. Gallagher. London: Karnac, 2002.

Lacan, J. (1966). *Écrits: The First Complete Edition in English*, trans. B. Fink. New York: W. W. Norton, 2006.

Lacan, J. (1993). *The Seminar of Jacques Lacan, Book 3: The Psychoses, 1955–1956*, ed. J.-A. Miller, trans. J. Forrester. New York: Norton.

Lacan, J. (2005). *On the Names of the Father*, trans. B. Fink. Malden, MA: Polity Press, 2013.

Lansky, M. R. (1992). *Fathers Who Fail*. Hillsdale, NJ: Analytic Press.

Laplanche, J. (1989). *New Foundations for Psychoanalysis*, trans. D. Macey. Oxford, UK: Basil Blackwell.

Laplanche, J. (1992). Interpretation between determinism and hermeneutics: a restatement of the problem. *Int. J. Psychoanal.*, 73:429–445.

Laplanche, J. (1997). The theory of seduction and the problem of the other. *Int. J. Psychoanal.*, 78:653–666.

Laplanche, J. (2007). Gender, sex, and the sexual. *Stud. Gender Sex.*, 8:201–219.

Laplanche, J. & Pontalis, J. B. (1973). *The Language of Psychoanalysis*, trans. D. Lagache. New York: Norton.

Lax, R. F. (1997). Boys' envy of mother and the consequences of this narcissistic mortification. *Psychoanal. Study Child*, 52:118–139.

Lemma, A. (2013). The body one has and the body one is: understanding the transsexual's need to be seen. *Int. J. Psychoanal.*, 94:277–292.

Lemma, A. (2018). Trans-itory identities: some psychoanalytic reflections on transgender identities. *Int. J. Psychoanal.*, 99:1089–1106.

Levinson, D. J., Darrow, C. N., Klein, E. B., Levinson, M. H. & McKee, B. (1978). *The Seasons of a Man's Life*. New York: Knopf.

Lewes, K. (1988). *The Psychoanalytic Theory of Male Homosexuality*. New York: Simon & Schuster.

Loewald, H. W. (1951). Ego and reality. *Int. J. Psychoanal.*, 32:10–18.

Loewald, H. W. (1962). Internalization, separation, mourning, and the superego. *Psychoanal. Q.*, 31:483–504.

Lyons-Ruth, K. (1991). Rapprochement or approchement: Mahler's theory reconsidered from the vantage point of recent research in early attachment relationships. *Psychoanal. Psychol.*, 8:1–23.

Maccoby, E. E. (1998). *The Two Sexes: Growing Apart, Coming Together*. Cambridge, MA: Harvard University Press.

Mahler, M. S., Pine, F. & Bergman, A. (1975). *The Psychological Birth of the Human Infant: Symbiosis and Individuation*. New York: Basic Books.

Manninen, V. (1992). The ultimate masculine striving: reflexions on the psychology of two polar explorers. *Scandinavian Psychoanal. Rev.*, 15:1–26.

Manninen, V. (1993). For the sake of eternity: on the narcissism of fatherhood and the father-son relationship. *Scandinavian Psychoanal. Rev.*, 16:35–46.

Marcus, B. F. & McNamara, S. (2013). Strange and otherwise unaccountable actions: category, conundrum, and trans identifies. *J. Amer. Psychoanal. Assn.*, 61:45–66.

Martel, M. M., Klump, K., Nigg, J. T., Breedlove, S. M. & Sisk, C. L. (2009). Potential hormonal mechanisms of attention-deficit/hyperactivity disorder and major depressive disorder: a new perspective. *Horm. Behav.*, 55:465–479.

Mayer, E. L. (1985). Everybody must be just like me: observations on female castration anxiety. *Int. J. Psychoanal.*, 66:331–347.

Mayer, E. L. (1991). Towers and enclosed spaces: a preliminary report on gender differences in children's reactions to block structures. *Psychoanal. Inquiry*, 11:480–510.

McClure, E. (2000). A meta-analytic review of sex differences in facial expression processing and their development in infants, children, and adolescents. *Psychol. Bull.*, 126:424–453.

McDougall, J. (1989). The dead father: on early psychic trauma and its relation to disturbance in sexual identity and in creative activity. *Int. J. Psychoanal.*, 70:205–219.

McWilliams, N. (1991). Mothering and fathering processes in the psychoanalytic art. *Psychoanal. Rev.*, 78:525–545.

Mitscherlich, A. (1969). *Society without the Father*, trans. E. Mosbacher. New York: Harcourt, Brace & World.

Money, J., Hampson, J. G. & Hampson, J. L. (1955). An examination of some basic concepts: the evidence of human hermaphroditism. *Bull. Johns Hopkins Hosp.*, 97:301–319.

Money, J., Hampson, J. G. & Hampson, J. L. (1957). Imprinting and the establishment of gender role. *AMA Arch. Neurol. Psychiatry*, 77:333–336.

Money-Kyrle, R. E. (1968). Cognitive development. *Int. J. Psychoanal.*, 49:691–698.

Moss, D. (2012). *Thirteen Ways of Looking at a Man: Psychoanalysis and Masculinity*. London: Routledge.

Neugarten, B. L. (1968). The awareness of middle age. In *Middle Age and Aging*. Chicago, IL: University of Chicago Press, pp. 93–98.

Ogden, T. H. (1989). *The Primitive Edge of Experience*. Northvale, NJ: Aronson.

Panksepp, J. (1998). *Affective Neuroscience: The Foundations of Human and Animal Emotions*. New York: Oxford University Press.

Parsons, M. (2007). Raiding the inarticulate: the internal analytic setting and listening beyond countertransference. *Int. J. Psychoanal.*, 88:1441–1456.

Perelberg, R. (2013). Paternal function and thirdness in psychoanalysis and legend: has the future been foretold? *Psychoanal. Q.*, 82:557–585.

Perelberg, R. (2015). *Murdered Father, Dead Father: Revisiting the Oedipus Complex*. London: Routledge.

Perelberg, R. J., ed. (2018). Introduction: a psychoanalytic understanding of bisexuality. In *Psychic Bisexuality: A British-French Dialogue*. London: Routledge, pp 1–57.

Person, E. & Ovesey, L. (1983). Psychoanalytic theories of gender identity. *J. Amer. Psychoanal. Assn.*, 11:203–226.

Phillips, S. (2001). The overstimulation of everyday life: new aspects of male homosexuality. *J. Amer. Psychoanal. Assn.*, 49:1235–1267.

Phillips, S. (2004). Homosexuality: coming out of the confusion. *Int. J. Psychoanal.*, 64:1431–1450.

Pollack, W. S. (1995). Deconstructing disidentification: rethinking psychoanalytic concepts of male development. *Psychoanal. Psychother.*, 12:30–45.

Pollack, W. S. (1998). *Real Boys: Rescuing Our Sons from the Myths of Boyhood*. New York: Random House.

Pruett, K. D. (1987). *The Nurturing Father*. New York: Warner Books.

Pruett, K. D. (1993). The paternal presence. *Fam. Soc.*, 74:46–50.

Pruyser, P. W. (1987). Creativity in aging persons. *Bull. Menninger Clin.*, 51:425–435.

Quindeau, I. (2013). Female sexuality beyond gender dichotomy. In *The Female Body: Inside and Outside*, ed. I. Moeslin-Teising & F. T. Salo. London: Karnac, pp. 223–242.

Redican, W. K. (1976). Adult male-infant interactions in nonhuman primates. In *The Role of the Father in Child Development*, ed. M. E. Lamb. New York: Wiley, pp. 345–385.

Reichbart, R. (2006). On men crying: Lear's agony. *J. Amer. Psychoanal. Assn.*, 54:1067–1098.

Reis, B. (2009). Names of the father. In *Heterosexual Masculinities*, ed. B. Reis & R. Grossmark. New York: Routledge, pp. 55–72.

Rose, J. (2016). Who do you think you are? *London Rev. Books*, 38:3–13.

Ross, J. M. (1975). The development of paternal identity: a critical review of the literature on generativity and nurturance in boys and men. *J. Amer. Psychoanal. Assn.*, 23:783–817.

Ross, J. M. (1977). Toward fatherhood: the epigenesis of paternal identity during a boy's first decade. *Int. Rev. Psychoanal.*, 4:327–347.

Ross, J. M. (1982). The roots of fatherhood: excursions into a lost literature. In *Father and Child*, ed. S. Cath, A. R. Gurwitt & J. M. Ross. Boston, MA: Little, Brown, pp. 3–20.

Ross, J. M. (1986). Beyond the phallic illusion: notes on man's heterosexuality. In *The Psychology of Men*, ed. G. Fogel, F. Lane & R. Liebert. New York: Basic Books, pp. 49–71.

Ross, J. M. (1990). The eye of the beholder: on the developmental dialogue between fathers and daughters. In *New Dimensions in Adult Development*, ed. R. A. Nemiroff & C. A. Colarusso. New York: Basic Books, pp. 47–72.

Salomonsson, B. (2014). *Psychoanalytic Therapy with Infants and Parents: Practice, Theory, and Results*. London: Routledge.

Sandler, J. (1976). Countertransference and role-responsiveness. *Int. Rev. Psychoanal.*, 3:43–47.

Sandman, C. A., Glynn, L. M. & Davis, E. P. (2013). Is there a viability-vulnerability tradeoff? Sex differences in fetal programming. *J. Psychosom. Res.*, 75:327–335.

Scarfone, D. (2019). The feminine, the analyst and the child theorist. *Int. J. Psychoanal.*, 100:567–575.

Schafer, R. (1968). *Aspects of Internalization*. New York: International Universities Press.

Schafer, R. (1974). Problems in Freud's psychology of women. *J. Amer. Psychoanal. Assn.*, 22:459–485.

Schalin, L. J. (1989). On phallicism: developmental aspects, neutralization, sublimation and defensive phallicism. *Scandinavian Psychoanal. Rev.*, 12:38–57.

Schiller, B.-M. (2012). Representing female desire within a labial framework of sexuality. *J. Amer. Psychoanal. Assn.*, 60:1161–1197.

Schiller, B.-M. (2018). Disillusioning gender. *J. Amer. Psychoanal. Assn.*, 66:243–261.

Seidman, S. & Frank, A. (2019). *Psychoanalysis and Contemporary American Men: Gender Identity in a Time of Uncertainty*. London: Routledge.

Spitz, R. (1956). Countertransference—comments on its varying role in the analytic situation. *J. Amer. Psychoanal. Assn.*, 4:256–265.

Sroufe, L. A., Egeland, B., Carlson, E. A. & Collins, W. A. (2005). *The Development of the Person: The Minnesota Study of Risk and Adaptation from Birth to Adulthood*. New York: Guilford Press.

Stein, R. (2002). Evil as love and as liberation. *Psychoanal. Dialogues*, 12:393–420.

Stein, R. (2003). Vertical mystical homoeros: an altered form of desire in fundamentalism. *Stud. Gender Sex.*, 4:38–58.

Stein, R. (2007). Moments in Laplanche's theory of sexuality. *Stud. Gender Sex.*, 8:177–200.

Steiner, J. (2011). *Seeing and Being Seen: Emerging from a Psychic Retreat*. London: Routledge.

Steiner, R. (1985). Turning a blind eye: the cover up for Oedipus. *Int. Rev. Psychoanal.*, 12:161–172.

Stern, D. N. (1985). *The Interpersonal World of the Infant: A View from Psychoanalysis and Developmental Psychology*. New York: Basic Books.

Stoller, R. J. (1964). A contribution to the study of gender identity. *Int. J. Psychoanal.*, 45:220–226.

Stoller, R. J. (1965). The sense of maleness. *Psychoanal. Q.*, 34:207–218.

Stoller, R. J. (1968). The sense of femaleness. *Psychoanal. Q.*, 37:42–55.

Stoller, R. J. (1976). Primary femininity. *J. Amer. Psychoanal. Assn.*, 24(suppl.): 58–78.

Stoller, R. J. (1985). *Presentations of Gender*. New Haven, CT: Yale University Press.

Sweetnam, A. (1996). The changing contexts of gender: between fixed and fluid experience. *Psychoanal. Dialogues*, 6:437–459.

Target, M. & Fonagy, P. (2002). Fathers in modern psychoanalysis and in society: the role of the father and child development. In *The Importance of Fathers: A Psychoanalytic Re-Evaluation*, ed. J. Trowell & A. Etchegoyen. London: Brunner-Routledge, pp. 45–66.

Teising, M. (2007). Narcissistic mortification of ageing men. *Int. J. Psychoanal.*, 88:1329–1344.

Teising, M. (2008). Am Lebensende zwischen narzisstischer Abwehr und facts of life. *Psychotherapie im Alter*, 2:201–212.

Tronick, E. (2007). *The Neurobehavioral and Social-Emotional Development of Infants and Children*. New York: W. W. Norton.

Tronick, E. & Reck, C. (2009). Infants of depressed mothers. *Harvard Rev. Psychiatry*, 17:147–156.

Tronick, E. & Weinberg, M. K. (2000). Gender differences and their relation to maternal depression. In *Stress, Coping, and Depression*, ed. S. L. Johnson, T. M. Field, N. Schneiderman & P. M. McCabe. Wahwah, NJ: Lawrence Erlbaum, pp. 23–34.

Tustin, F. (1987). *Autistic Barriers in Neurotic Patients*. London: Karnac.

Weinberg, M. K., Olson, K. L., Beeghly, M. & Tronick, E. Z. (2006). Making up is hard to do, especially for mothers with high levels of depressive symptoms and their infant sons. *J. Child Psychol. Psychiatry*, 47:670–683.

Weinberg, M. K., Tronick, E. Z., Cohn, J. F. & Olson, K. L. (1999). Gender differences in emotional expressivity and self-regulation during early infancy. *Dev. Psychol.*, 35:175–188.

Whitman, W. (1855). *Leaves of Grass.* New York: Penguin, 1986.

Wilkinson, S. (2001). Sexual agency as an alternative to the boy's dis-identification from mother. Paper presented at the Spring Meeting of the Division of Psychoanalysis (39) of the American Psychological Association, Santa Fe, NM, April.

Winnicott, D. W., ed. (1956). Primary maternal preoccupation. In *Collected Papers: Through Paediatrics to Psycho-Analysis.* New York: Basic Books, 1958, pp. 300–305.

Winnicott, D. W. (1960). The theory of the parent-infant relationship. *Int. J. Psychoanal.*, 41:585–595.

Winnicott, D. W. (1964). *The Child, the Family, and the Outside World.* New York: Penguin Books.

Winnicott, D. W. (1965). *The Maturational Processes and the Facilitating Environment: Studies in the Theory of Emotional Development.* London: Hogarth.

Winnicott, D. W. (1971). *Playing and Reality.* London: Tavistock.

Winnicott, D. W. (1980). *The Piggle: An Account of the Psychoanalytic Treatment of a Little Girl*, ed. I. Ramzy. London: Hogarth.

Wisdom, J. (1983). Male and female. *Int. J. Psychoanal.*, 64:159–168.

Wrye, H. & Welles, J. K. (1994). *The Narration of Desire: Erotic Transferences and Countertransferences.* Hillsdale, NJ: Analytic Press.

Young-Eisendrath, P. (1997). Gender and contrasexuality: Jung's contribution and beyond. In *The Cambridge Companion to Jung*, ed. P. Young-Eisendrath & T. Dawson. Cambridge, UK: Cambridge University Press, pp. 223–239.

Zeanah, C. H., Egger, H. L., Smyke, A. T., Nelson, C. A., Fox, N. A., Marshall, P. J. & Guthrie, D. (2009). Institutional rearing and psychiatric disorders in Romanian preschool children. *Amer. J. Psychiatry*, 166:777–785.

Zweibel, R. (2004). The third position: reflections about the internal analytic working process. *Psychoanal. Q.*, 73:215–265.

Index

For Product Safety Concerns and Information please contact our EU
representative GPSR@taylorandfrancis.com
Taylor & Francis Verlag GmbH, Kaufingerstraße 24, 80331 München, Germany

www.ingramcontent.com/pod-product-compliance
Lightning Source LLC
Chambersburg PA
CBHW070346270326
41926CB00017B/4014